With all

Sylvia

xxxx

25/12/84

Jock Tamson's Bairns

Jock Tamson's Bairns

ESSAYS ON A SCOTS CHILDHOOD

EDITED BY

TREVOR ROYLE

'the human race, common humanity, also with less
sentimental force, a group of people united by a
common sentiment, interest or purpose.'
Scottish National Dictionary, Volume Five

HAMISH HAMILTON
LONDON

First published in Great Britain 1977
by Hamish Hamilton Ltd
90 Great Russell Street London WC1B 3PT

This collection copyright © *Trevor Royle 1977*

SBN 241 89638 x

Printed in Great Britain by
Bristol Typesetting Co Ltd
Barton Manor, St Philips, Bristol

For Sebastian, George and Patrick
that they may know what it was like

Contents

Preface

Youth is a common currency for us all and yet it is in our pasts, wherever we may have spent them, that we are able to see the influences that have helped to mould our lives. All the writers who have contributed to this book about a Scots childhood have one thing in common—each was brought up and educated in Scotland. And yet each has a different story to tell. Scotland is a small country with the majority of the population crammed into its central belt. Outside that are areas as various as the Highland communities of the north and north-west which have little in common with the agricultural and fishing peoples of the north-east. Similarly the industrial west, the scar tissue of the country's past, belongs to a different world from the reasoned eighteenth-century landscape of East Lothian. Everywhere one looks, the country and its people have different faces to show to the world.

Children growing up in such varying and disparate backgrounds found a kinship in education. It is education, too, that provides a unity to this book. Education in Scotland is different, not only because the system differs from that in England and Wales but also because the Scottish attitudes to education are almost unique. Education in the 1950s had not changed its basic philosophy since the days of the village dominies who gave all-round educations to the lads o' pairts, those splendid eighteenth- and nineteenth-century gentlemen who had an equal and solid grounding in the arts and sciences. The scale might have been smaller in the days of the dominies but an awesome attitude towards education persisted in our childhoods, a belief that children had to go to school to be taught what work meant and what attitudes of behaviour and belief they had to respect. There remained a deep-rooted insistence at all levels of society (of the twelve writers, three went to public schools, the rest educated within the state system, two are English, one a native Gaelic

A*

speaker) that children must go to school to better themselves and —above all—to get on.

Other influences peculiar to Scotland assert themselves. Religion tends to run education a close second, not because it was a childhood pre-occupation, but because it was receding dramatically and had all but lost its once pervasive influence. Knox and Calvin hardly touched our lives in a direct way—it is too easy to say that they suppressed the Scottish people and tormented the national psyche. In the terms of our childhoods we were left with their legacy of an impressive belief in learning for its own sake, a foundation for scholarship added to a strong vein of scepticism and a necessity for an ordered framework to life itself.

This is a book, too, about Scotland seen through the eyes of those who were children in the 1950s. There is always a tendency to see one's past in the less than honest terms of fond remembrance, and as a nation we are drawn too easily to the backward glance and to the sentimental attachment to events long past. We trust that we have avoided that pitfall here and that we are near to the truth of the Scotland that our collective pasts remember. At a time when the country is facing up to the facts of devolution and long-lost and half-forgotten feelings of nationhood are again rising to the surface it would perhaps be tempting to see in these essays yet another investigation of the Scottish soul. That should be resisted. We cannot change what we once were and what is told here is only part of the story. Another kind of book will be needed to tell us where we are now going.

TREVOR ROYLE
Edinburgh, December 1976

ALAN BOLD

Confessions of an Escapologist

And yet boldness is a child of ignorance and baseness.

Francis Bacon, *Essays*

First—what else?—a literary anecdote by way of introduction. In 1969 I had reason to feel I was making some kind of general impact as a poet, for that year Chatto and Windus brought out two collections of mine (*A Perpetual Motion Machine* and *The State of the Nation*) while a selection of my work was included in *Penguin Modern Poets 15*. By the slimly voluminous standards of poetry-publishing that was quite a splash, a couple of drops in the ocean. However poetry is part of the lives of very few people, so when my local Edinburgh grocer asked me what I was currently up to and I told him he gave me one of 'yon' kind of looks. 'You a writer then?' he asked. When I said I was he was even more sceptical. 'You met Sir Compton Mackenzie then?' was his second, more loaded, question. Now he delivered groceries to Sir Compton at his home in Drummond Place—about five minutes walk from my flat in Gayfield Square—and when I admitted I had not met Sir Compton the grocer observed that I could not be much of a writer. He was displaying the cautious empiricism built into the bones of every Scot (from David Hume downwards). This requires a proof for every assertion. I might kid on I was a writer but nobody was going to take that for granted. It was not the end of the story.

When, shortly after the publication of *The State of the Nation*, I was interviewed for the *Sunday Times* by Philip Oakes, I repeated my grocer story as a cautionary tale of being brought down to earth in Scotland. As a result of this public disclosure I was invited by Sir Compton to come round to see him. Naturally I was flattered. I was twenty-six and he was eighty-six. I was a complete beginner; he was a household name so illustrious that the general public would pay good money to read about his life and times as

1

they unfolded octave by octave. Feeling a bit apprehensive about confronting such a legend I fortified myself beforehand with a quarter-bottle of Bells (not whisky galore exactly but sufficient to put me at my ease) and walked round to Drummond Place, accompanied by my wife, and knocked at his door.

Sir Compton sat surrounded by books and an aura of distinction. He did most of the talking and I was treated to a virtuoso display of his phenomenal gift of total recall. He remembered every detail of his childhood almost, it seemed, since the moment of conception and recounted it lovingly. It was a privileged background, sweet to the memory. It was also a teleological story: that is, his life was the pleasantly inevitable extension of a comfortable initial situation. Everything that happened to him was implied in his childhood like a smooth solution of Wordsworth's paradox of the child being father of the man. Unused to mixing with such fine folk as Sir Compton I was intimidated when he asked me about *my* childhood. I shrugged my shoulders feeling my past would be too squalid for his finely attuned ears. Still, we have it on the authority of the later Wittgenstein that a shrug can be meaningful so what follows is what that shrug meant.

Growing up in Scotland—at least until the age of fifteen—prepared me for precisely nothing, though the way of life moulded me. I was not encouraged in any direction, was not aware of the supposed joys of Scottish education, was not blessed with any feeling of domestic security. Which is not to say I learned nothing. On the contrary I received an impression so strong as to be indelible. It was that people are visibly conditioned by the physical reality of their early environment. The educational system—at least as it existed then—did nothing to liberate the unprivileged child but rather reinforced his limitations. Sartre's philosophical insistence that the individual constitutes his own freedom and can obtain it by asserting his existential independence has thus always seemed to me to be an academic attitude rather than a step on the road to freedom. It simply ignores the way in which consciousness can be distorted by an ambiance of ignorance and limited by economic circumstances. As it is impossible to shake off the shaping experience of childhood it follows that until there is an end to economic and cultural underprivilege there will be no real beginning for millions of people. For them the occasional explosion of violence will have to compensate for the lack of conversational equipment.

I was born in Edinburgh on April 20, 1943. Thus I shared a birthday with Hitler and was ripped untimely from my mother's womb—by Caesarian operation—and delivered to a world that the German birthday boy had ensured would be uncertain. I lived in the same flat at 19 Gayfield Square for thirty-two years. It was a typical working class flat in a typical working class tenement and existence was a hand-to-mouth affair. On my thirtieth birthday, sitting in that flat and looking out towards Fife (where I now live) over the corrugated roofs of a familiar garage, I wrote a poem, 'Autobiography', to express my feelings of stagnating in that flat and imposing it on my wife and daughter:

I have observed the same stones for thirty years.
Studied various cloudcreations in those squares

Of dull confusion. Wishing for green skies in blue seas
I have instead cheated my eyes on browns and greys

And the rigidity of rooftops with corrugations that
Mock the way blown water laps. Often I have sat

Gazing at the belly of the atmosphere, watched
A star fizzle or a bird fly, been bewitched

By the things shade can do, the way that light
Can fall on things you only fear at night.

I have imprisoned myself in four small rooms
And decayed there. Others crave homes

But I have retained the selfsame slot
With voices underneath and above the feet

Of another trapped family. Worse, I have
Imposed this sentence on those I love.

Now that I have left that flat for good (I use the word in a qualitative sense) it is instructive to see how I came to such a melancholy conclusion.

For various reasons my father had to be away from home most of the time—mainly in the Orkneys where he worked as a clerk of works because, after smashing his arm in a car crash, he could no longer hold his own as a joiner. So I shared that flat with my mother, my brother Billy (four years older than me and destined to become a paratrooper) and my mother's two brothers John (a plumber) and Dodo (a baker). My father had been divorced which taught me that marriages were brittle enough to be easily broken. My mother had to work as my father spent so much of his wages on the 'sin' (the Sunday school called it that) of drinking that there was little left to send to Edinburgh. My mother worked by 'doing' for middle class women who were too languid to tidy their own homes. Naturally we were led to believe that these middle class people were a cut above the likes of us. They lived in a different world. For my part I grew up with the knowledge that we were a poor family. It was not so much that meals were invariably fried or that clothes were handed down. It was more the deadness of the house, the lack of conversational brightness, the avuncular boorishness, the ubiquitous hostility. Basically it was the acceptance of defeat. Always, always, always I wanted to escape from this defeatism.

The climate of defeat extended into school. I went to London Street Primary, a little school round the corner, and the whole point of the education there was to keep us firmly in our places—to 'teach' us to be completely subservient to the staff. To this end we were exposed to a bunch of sadistic mediocrities who heaped indignities on children whose parents were too timid to do anything about it. It started with a diminutive spinster who hit us with a ruler for daring to talk. Then there was a gym teacher whose method of punishment was to ask offenders to place their heads between his outstretched palms—which then closed with a resounding smack on the offending head. There was a male deputy headmaster who strutted round school with a Nietzschean moustache and his 'belt' (tawse) tucked under the left shoulder of his shabby chalky tweed jacket so he could produce it, with a flourish, at any moment. The sounds I most remember from that school are the deadening Souza tunes we kids had to march upstairs to, and the sound of children being hammered on the hands by twisted adults. Since then I have been totally opposed to corporal punishment because of its ritualised irrationality, and because its spurious legality of *in loco parentis* grotesquely assumes that it is normal for parents to assault their children.

For me then life began when I could escape from school and escape from the house. Happiness was getting out of school; it was playing in the streets; it was taking the girls down to the cellar gang huts and having marathon kissing competitions; it was watching Hibs win the Scottish League two years running in 1950-1 and 1951-2; it was gang skirmishes with the Montgomery

4

Street lads; it was collecting for the bonfire on firework night; it was breaking windows and running away from the staff at Gayfield Square police station; it was getting away from the tedium of uncles John and Dodo; it was cycling down to Portobello Pool in the summer and swimming for hours and eating shivery bites; it was helping the milkman on his horse-driven cart; it was smoking surreptitious 'joysticks' (fags the length of three ordinary cigarettes); it was trips to Dunbar with my cousin Teddie and her husband Mickey; it was everything non-scholastic, non-domestic. As for the church—which is supposed to throw a big black shadow over the lives of all Scots—it did not matter a damn. Religion was singing boring hymns in school and sniggering through 'Onward Christian Soldiers'. Or it was stories at Sunday school.

Nevertheless I remember one experience that hovered on the periphery of religion. My principal childhood fantasy was imagining I was really Superman, that bizarre comic-strip character who could do unto others as he bleeding well wanted to. I loved the idea of the mild Clark Kent being metamorphosed into an indestructible hero. I would dress up, when nobody else was in the house, with pyjamas, swimming trunks and a towel tucked into my collar—like a flowing flying cloak. I thought I was the spitting image of Superman in this clobber. Then I would jump off chairs and dream I was soaring through the sky, escaping from everything. One day I was quite sure I had actually flown for an instant and this tempted me to contemplate springing off the window-sill from our third-storey flat and surging into an escapist wild blue yonder. Then I thought of an incident from the Bible I had been reluctantly moved by at Sunday school. It is the passage from Matthew 27 which runs: 'Likewise also the chief priests mocking him, with the scribes and elders, said, He saved others; himself he cannot save. If he be the King of Israel, let him now come down from the cross, and we will believe him'.

If only Christ *had* come down and escaped from that cross, I remember thinking. Then there would be a world of miraculous escapes from the inevitable defeat. If only he could have thrown off his tragic passivity and, Superman-like, swooped down and scattered all his foes—then religion might have been more than a pie-in-the-sky tabloid tale told by four unreliable reporters (Matthew, Mark, Luke and John: hold that cuddy till I get on). But no—Christ's message was the acceptance of suffering. He was part of the defeat. If Christ had, in that story, come down from

5

the cross I am certain that that day I would have jumped from the window-sill and God knows what might have happened. I put one leg out on the window-ledge, looked down and thought: perhaps Jesus, the official Superman, will help me jump. But I remembered: *He saved others; himself he cannot save.* There was no miraculous escape from that house. It was going to be on my back for some time to come.

Such private fantasies I kept, wisely, strictly to myself. They would have sounded soft to my pals and to survive in working class Edinburgh you had to appear tough. I say *appear* tough because some of the most cowardly lads disguised their diffidence by cursing and swearing and sounding tough. It was cowardice, too, that led to the formation of gangs—the whole concept is the abnegation of the individual—and our Gayfield Square Gang was no exception. Humble at heart we pretended to despise those we envied: the kids in posh school uniforms who passed through our territory on their way home to comfort. One typical day we victimised a schoolboy of a more elevated social status. He was walking past us unsuspectingly when we pounced on him—about ten of us—took off his cap, then tied him to the railings near a garage. He was howling and we were laughing at his misery. It was a commonplace kind of occurrence. When, years later, that same boy drowned in a sailing accident and I heard the news I instantly visualised his stricken vulnerable expression as he stood there helpless before a jeering group of morons. We were, in many ways, a despicable bunch of kids: cruel, insensitive on principle, thoughtless and arrogant with our ignorance. Instead of fighting against our predicament we fought each other.

At school I preferred to watch fights rather than taking part in them. However one day a school bully—he had attained his bully-boy status more because, being prematurely large, he looked the part than for any demonstrable fistic ability—challenged me outside the elm tree that stands in the playground of London Street school. This happened continually and it was impossible to back down because thereafter life would not have been worth living. Those who conceded defeat without a fight were soft touches ever afterwards. When the bully came at me with his big menacing paws I thumped him on the left ear and his ear blushed scarlet and his big mouth sagged in astonishment and pain. Intuitively grasping that my opponent was finished if he could not terrify by his presence, I banged him on the same ear again. And

6

again and again. He began to 'bubble' (cry) and I was cheered. Impressed by my hollow triumph I saw a new escape into the realms of championship boxing.

The upshot of my playground victory was that I went, with two pals, to enrol at the Sparta Boxing Club in MacDonald Road. Far from being a platform to instant fame the club turned out to be a centre for hard graft. The evening sessions started with endless press-ups and punching exercises and only after what seemed like an agony of effort did the actual boxing begin. Then came the moment of truth. After a couple of supervised bouts I realised that technical ability counted for more than strength for it was possible to be ridiculed by some wee bloke who could dance and weave around you and stick out jabs and throw fast hooks and deliver devastating uppercuts. Few of us got the chance to shine, anyway, because there was one outstanding boy there. His name was Kenny Buchanan and he was dedicated and brilliant with the most potent straight left I have ever seen, a left like a piston. Although I hardly knew him then I felt an immense surge of vicarious pride when years later Ken won the lightweight championship of the world.

Crazily enough it was the connection—however ignominious on my part—with the Sparta that led to my first memorable encounter with sex. There was a girl called Nancy in Gayfield Square (at least I called her Nancy in a poem called 'A Night's Dream' in *Penguin Modern Poets 15*). For her age she was phenomenally well developed and, being rather slow on the uptake mentally, she learned how to make her presence felt by emphasising her superb mammary glands. Now, as my visits to the Sparta were becoming more and more infrequent I devised a plan to engage the sympathy of Nancy as I was pretty sure she would believe anything. My mother had some steel-hinged hair grips that snapped open and shut with sharp metallic teeth. I fastened them on my knuckles one night and scratched the skin until it bled. That accomplished, I strode into the street and saw the omnipresent Nancy. It was early evening and it had been raining and the low sun sparkled on the cobble stones.

'Going to the boxing, Alan?' Nancy asked. Black hair. Large full mouth. She exuded sensuousness. 'Can't,' I told her abruptly and showed her the lacerated knuckles. 'I did this sparring with my bare hands.' A complete lie but Nancy was not one to suspect mendacity. For the life of me I don't know why I expected her to be impressed by my self-imposed wounds but she was. 'What a shame,' she pouted as she had seen film stars do. And I sighed at the thought of her body. I suggested we talk down in the cellars away from the wet. This was not in itself a sinister suggestion so we went down and lit a candle in these dank underground cellars and we talked. Mainly about her breasts. She had a primitive brassière on which made a sort of straight ledge of her tits.

'Is that their real shape,' I enquired all-innocent like. 'No, there's a space in the middle here'—and she pushed the sweater into her profound cleavage. 'Can I feel?' I asked, dry-lipped, hungry with anticipation. ' Yes,' she answered with a little smile and flash of her big brown eyes. That was the signal for action. I ran my hands over her breasts and we both started kissing. I got my hands inside the cups of her heavy-duty brassière and felt the wonderfully malleable contours of her warm flesh. She began to get worried. 'Stop, Alan, that's enough.' But I hadn't had enough and I stroked and caressed her, felt myself suffused with her magical femininity. 'No,' she started to push me away, 'my mother wouldn't like that.'

O Christ! That did it! Her mother!!!!! A sudden mental picture of her mother—whose devotion to poking her nose out of the window in search of gossip earned her the nickname 'News of the World'—brought me to a standstill. I was still excited but the ecstasy had gone. However I had grasped the shape of things to come. Sexual excitement offered an intense, if transient, escape from the present and I intended to utilise this particular escape route at every possible opportunity. Beyond the grottiness of the street and the unimaginative people in it the very fact of sex demonstrated that there was a passionate dimension available to everyone. So everyone could, from time to time, escape from the pressure of everyday defeat.

At the age of eleven two things were foremost in my mind. Thanks to Nancy, one of them was the realisation of the liberating power of sex. The other was the imminent qualifying examination for secondary school. If a pupil did tolerably well in the 'qualie' he or she went to the local Senior Secondary School. If he or she did less well—and this was the majority—then he or she went to the Junior Secondary. As my brother was already at the Senior Secondary, Broughton, I was in a position to know the main difference between the two types of schooling was that the self-styled 'higher' education involved boys playing rugby. At the

8

Junior Secondary—or local was Bellevue—the kids were allowed to get on with football. Like all my pals I wanted to go to the football-playing school. The idea of planning a career never entered my tiny mind.

The real idea of the institution of rugby at the Senior Secondary was, of course, to give a shabby simulation of the public (i.e. private) school atmosphere. Rugby-playing boys had always been socially superior to the fitba'-daft lads so entrance to the Senior Secondary was like getting a foot on the bottom rung of the social ladder. We had, in one examination, to demonstrate our fitness for either football or rugby. When the results were announced I learned, with horror, that I had been selected for a rugby-playing education. I was dismayed and in the eyes of my pals I was a treacherous bastard, for they all received notice to go to Bellevue. I felt cut off, a misfit in my own backyard. It was rootless enough living in a slummy urban environment. To be isolated within that environment was sheer hell. When my father, up in Orkney, was informed of my achievement he decided to come to Edinburgh so he could extricate my brother and me from Gayfield Square and treat us to a summer in Orkney.

My father arrived in a taxi: the door opened and he staggered out. He was pissed out of his mind, but this was nothing new for the few times I had seen him it had been thus. He got through Saturday in an alcoholic haze and on Sunday I went to the local paper-shop for our sabbath reading. I said the same thing to the newspaper-man every Sunday, all in one breath: *News of the World, Sunday Post, Sunday Dispatch* and *The Reynolds*. As always the *Sunday Post* was my favourite because its pull-out Fun Section contained several features conceived and illustrated by Dudley D. Watkins whose crude cross-hatched draughtsmanship is to this day the visual art most familiar to Scottish working class kids. I read about 'Oor Wullie': that unkempt dungaree-clad street-urchin forever kicking footballs through windows and collecting black eyes—'keekers'—in fights. And I read about 'The Broons' whose huge family included gallant Pa, hard-man Joe, big drip Hen, and specky swot Horace. I dreaded that going to Broughton might make me like the universally despised Horace.

Eventually we left for Orkney, getting the train up north and then a boat that took us sailing idyllically into Stromness harbour where a little crowd stood waving at the new arrivals. From Stromness it was on to Kirkwall thence to Dounby Farm where my

9

father lived in a little wooden cabin. I remember that period in Orkney as a liquid golden summer full of gentle animals and warm people and fields that shook gently in the sun. It was the one stretch of unmitigated pleasure in my childhood. Here was a genuine escape from urban defeatism. Here people seemed a part of their environment, not apart from it. Whether we were out fishing on the lakes or exploring the remains of Skara Brae or working on the farm there was a purpose and a satisfaction in everything. Life in Edinburgh meant passing time. Here the unique coalescence of past and present imparted a glorious feeling of timelessness. Orkney, that summer, was like a dream but a dream that had more solid beauty than the repetitive reality of the streets of Edinburgh. I didn't ever want to go back. But I had to. Back to the back streets. Back to the boredom of Gayfield Square. Back to Broughton Senior Secondary School.

If anything Broughton was more deadly dull than London Street. Children were streamed into grades of estimated ability and I went straight into the bottom C stream. I quickly associated myself with the roughest lot in my class and together we put up a sustained resistance to schooling. The one hard fact was that I had three years to get through before I could leave school and I determined to do as little as possible as if a studied indolence could constitute an escape. After the summer in Orkney I felt permanently depressed. Then, in January 1956, something exciting happened: the emergence of a voice that gave a massive, pulsating V-sign to the school, to the street, to urban defeatism. Elvis Presley's 'Heartbreak Hotel' was released and I became an instant convert to rock. My new escape would be to ape Elvis. He was exotic, yet closer to my heart than anything within immediate grasp. He was anathema to those in authority. Parents and teachers—the dreaded 'them'—hated him and I liked him all the more for that.

I managed to get a cheap guitar—which I painted black—and slicked my hair in Elvis fashion. He became my God, something to believe in, someone whose immense panache could transcend the dullness of Gayfield Square. Pictures of Elvis—cut from magazines —became instant icons and I scrutinised them religiously. For the first time I put my mind to something: becoming the greatest local authority on Elvis Presley. I remember clearly standing at the bottom of the stair and impressing the girls, including the nearest available Nancy, with my new-found Presleyan erudition. The world suddenly seemed a better place. Identification with Elvis

10

gave me a cockiness too. One teacher asked me to explain to the class what was so wonderful about this American singer and I found I *could* communicate something of the intense excitement I felt. The teacher thought I was stupid or wicked or worse but as far as I was concerned the teacher could go jump in a lake.

Two months after the release of 'Heartbreak Hotel', in a silent little water-filled quarry in Orkney, my father was found drowned. I was shattered. I did not know why he had drowned but I knew that it had happened, that he had chosen to die away from his family. He had escaped into oblivion. All my instincts had made me a 'loner' but this distant death confirmed vividly that I was indeed alone. There could be no escape from this solitude. The impact on my thirteen-year-old mind was immense. The holiday in Orkney had been like a reprieve from my predicament. Now there was nothing: no future, no reunion in Orkney, no nothing. There I was, a pathetic *ersatz* Elvis crying in the Scottish wilderness.

Rather than show my grief I became as intolerable as possible. I dressed outrageously and behaved stupidly. Cultivating a nasty exterior I showed contempt for my teachers and they seemed to hate me. I rationalised that my lack of formal education was simply reciprocating the indifference shown to me by the teachers who were, or thought they were, superior people because of their salaried respectability. One female teacher, a French mistress, told us that we in the C stream were 'fish-and-chippers': types whose abysmally low mentality would never rise above the odour of Scotland's national *alfresco* dish. Well, we were Scottish and not French (where's yer French fries now, then!) so it seemed appropriate to contort our features in the face of Scotland's worst characteristic—aggressive negativity.

When I at last attained the school-leaving age of fifteen I felt my moment had come. I was glad to see the back of Broughton and the feeling was mutual. This would be my big escape into life. At last I had my freedom. Yet that freedom turned out to be the freedom to do one of a handful of hideously boring jobs. That kind of intolerably limited freedom is merely the freedom to choose between bad and evil. I chose bad. Most of the summer after leaving school was spent lying in Gayfield Square gardens perusing the Situations Vacant column of the *Edinburgh Evening News*. One thing was sure—my miraculous escape from the sensation of defeat was not going to come this way. I was going to become another face in the faceless crowd.

11

My first job was as a petrol pump attendant and I lasted for a few weeks. I kept forgetting to screw the petrol cap back after I had filled the tank and irate customers would come back and verbally abuse me before reporting me to the boss. Those who have done manual jobs during a 'varsity vac' find them 'an experience'. They have their heads above water—I felt I was drowning in my own impotent rage. To work for a man who has the power of hire and fire over you fills you with a feeling of utter helplessness. When the garage fired me there was nothing I could do but brood about it.

After the garage I got a job, through the Youth Employment Exchange, as an apprentice baker. I thought this would be a piece of cake but it turned out to be a voluntary exercise in mental atrophy. When sensible folk were still asleep I cycled to work in the dawn to stand by a conveyor belt so I could stick lids on to pies that were heading for the oven. There were variations on the bakery theme: I might help inside a large refrigerated room then stand at the end of a hot oven and swelter to pile trays of sausage rolls into a tall trolley. Here, too, I saw defeatism in action. The men and women who worked at the bakery accepted everything that life flung in their faces. They accepted industrial accidents with equanimity, accepted empty marriages, accepted small wage packets, accepted that this was life. Their great escape was the weekend boozeup. I saw the prospect of becoming like that, of becoming like my uncle Dodo (now extinct).

I wanted to escape from this—but what could I escape into? Another job, given my lack of qualifications, would present the same problems. On the other hand unemployment would be a slow death. I had plenty of time to think in the intellectually un-demanding bakery and I thought a lot. I thought that my feeling of inadequacy derived from the fact that I could not accept other people's assessment of me. There was, I felt, more to me than met their eyes. I had something to say but was too inarticulate to set it down. If I could remedy that I might begin to get somewhere. The obvious difference between myself and those who dismissed me was they they were educated and I had trained myself to be pig ignorant. Before I could achieve anything I would have to educate myself and the only place I could get time to do that was—at school. It was an appalling admission but there was no escape from it. No escape from myself and what I thought I could amount to.

12

Impulsively I chucked my job at the bakery and wrote to Broughton asking if they would have me back. The headmaster, Robert J. Walker, told me that the staff did not want me back under any circumstances but that he was willing to take the responsibility for the return of the prodigal. I assured him that I had come to realise that education was the only genuine escape from defeatism, only it wasn't really an escape but a way of confronting life on equal terms. He told me that it would mean a complete change of attitude, that I would be going back to the drawing board. I had let fifteen years escape me and from now on I, not my environmental limitations, would have to be in control. I went back, went on to university, became a writer and painter: whether I have proved anything or not is for others to say.

'Escapism' has become a dirty word but it is basically clean in concept. If your environment grips you like a prison the honourable thing to do is escape from it. If more of us realise that the typically anti-social anti-cultural working class environment is an oppressive prison then we can begin to do something about setting the prisoners at large armed with the knowledge of what liberty means.

ALAN SPENCE

Boom Baby

There were twenty-seven thousand of us born in Glasgow that year—1947, two years after the war, and the baby-boom in full spate.

My father was a sailmaker, but was soon to lose his job. My mother had worked in a bakery before her pregnancy. I was the third son to be born to them, and the only one to survive more than a few days.

Pushed out from the mothering warmth I was part of, into harshness of light and noise, roughness and hard sharp edges, pain of separation, pain of the fall, 'trailing clouds of glory', I arrived. Grey Glasgow December and freezing cold. But I made it through the winter. I was named. I existed as a separate individual.

Those earliest years come back to me sometimes as a vague déjà vu, a sense of something lost. The sweet comfort of my mother's breast, the close warm smells, the gentle rock and shoogle of travelling in a pram.

I remember lying on a blanket, on what I can now name as a shingle beach, and being one with it, each pebble, the sea and the sky. All me. All not-me. And looking back now, it seems my childhood and adolescence were like a steady movement away from that state, towards separativity, fragmentation, alienation.

There were great hopes for us, that new generation. Vera Lynn had been singing it during the war.

> 'There'll be love and laughter
> And joy ever after
> Tomorrow
> When the world is new . . .'

My new world was a room and kitchen with a narrow lobby in between. The kitchen was where we really lived. There we ate, we washed at the sink, we slept in a big box-bed where I curled at

14

my parents' feet. We didn't use the room much, except in summer. It cost too much to keep room and kitchen heated.

We were on the top floor of the tenement—'three up right'—and the room window looked out to the front, across a lemonade factory opposite, over rows and rows of other tenements, towards the jutting cranes of the shipyards and the docks. The kitchen window looked out on to the back court. Beyond that was a Corporation yard, then a stretch of waste-ground bounded by factories, and behind that Ibrox Stadium, the press-box perched like a little castle on top of the stand. Further away again, just visible through a gap between buildings, were trees in Bellahouston Park —glimpse of a magic place, distant and green. Sometimes in summer we would go there on a Sunday afternoon, a great expedition across two main roads. In the park I would run and tumble and my father would try to teach me how to kick a ball. We would go to hear the brass bands in the bandstand, not paying to go in but listening from the hillside above. I can still remember the quality of the light on those summer evenings, almost a sadness in it, my father perhaps carrying me on his shoulder, coming home.

When I was eventually allowed to go out and play on my own, the back spaces were my kingdom—the back court, the yard, the wasteground. There were gaps in the railings leading through to other backs, other worlds. There were other children to play with or fight with. There were walls to climb, middens and bomb-shelters to explore.

One winter I fell sick with scarlet fever, caught, I was told, through rummaging in middens, playing in puddles that were sometimes green and stagnant. And in my parents' sympathy and concern, there was nevertheless an element of exasperation. They had warned me about playing in the muck. I had brought the sickness on myself. I was a midden-raker, a dirty boy.

I spent that Christmas in hospital. I remember lying there in the dim ward, paper decorations on the ceiling, and an older boy calling out to me from the next bed. He asked if I was a Protestant or a Catholic. I didn't know. I had never heard the words before. He laughed at that, thought I was stupid. Then he asked if I supported Rangers or Celtic. 'Rangers,' I said, thinking of the little castle on the roof of Ibrox stadium. 'Well then,' he said. 'Ye must be a Protestant. That's OK.'

When I got home I asked my parents about Protestants and

15

Catholics, but they weren't able to explain, in any way I could understand, just what the words meant, or what the difference was between them.

My parents also had spells in hospital around that time, my mother with attacks of asthma and bronchitis, my father with a recurring skin disease that put his job in jeopardy.

When my mother was ill, I was sent for the first time to a Corporation Nursery school. The nursery was called Merryland, after the street where it was located, but I also like to think there was a consciousness, however ironic, of what the name meant. A merry land.

At first I hated the change, the imprisonment. On my way out to the school in the mornings, I would see other boys out playing in the back, and I envied them their freedom. The nursery was clean and ordered. We queued up every morning for doses of cod-liver oil, orange juice and rose-hip syrup. A whole generation of us were weaned on them.

'... Wo ho, Glory Hallelujah
Cod-liver oil and the orange juice ...'

But I adapted to the new reality, accepted it as normal. The nursery itself was a pleasant place. Walled in from the outside world, it had a garden, of sorts, a back lawn and a sandpit. Inside there was a hall where we played games and painted pictures, danced and learned songs. I made new friends, and enemies. I fell in love with three wee girls, all at once. My assertive little ego came up against others just as tyrannical as itself, and I had to accommodate. I became part of a community.

I have no idea how long I was there; a year perhaps, or more. But in child's time it was forever.

Eventually though, I was old enough to move on to Primary school. That was to be a whole new phase, another reality again, and one I found much harder to accept.

The Primary school was in amongst those tenements that led down to the docks. It was built of the same grey stone, a three-storey block with an asphalt playground. The change from nursery school was dramatic and frightening. Loud bells jangled us in and out of the place. We were regimented, lined up, marched here and there. The rooms were huge and dismal; there were forty or fifty of us in a class; and the teacher was a great thundering

16

woman always shouting at us. SIT UP straight. FOLD your arms. STOP talking. YOU!

Her first task, it seemed, was to break our spirits, and two incidents in those early days reduced me to despair.

The first began one day in the playground when I needed to empty my bladder. Without giving it a thought, I started to piss against the wall. Two little girls from my class started pointing at me and laughing, and I turned, tiny cock in hand, and squirted at them. They ran off, saying they would tell the teacher, and they did, as soon as we went inside.

The teacher took me out of the classroom and told me what a filthy disgusting creature I was. I had been so bad in fact that she wouldn't punish me herself, but would send me to the headmaster to be dealt with. As it happened, the headmaster was more lenient. He ranted, but he didn't belt me. I slunk back to the classroom and sat in misery for the rest of the day. The worst thing was that I didn't feel I could tell my parents. I had been bad, and for all I knew they might punish me more. I wanted to hide away, to disappear. I had eaten of the tree of the knowledge of good and evil. I was ashamed. I knew guilt.

The second incident was even worse, and came just a week later. We had each been issued with paper and a box of wax crayons, and I had been happily drawing, lost in it. At the end of the day the teacher said 'All right, you can take these home.' I thought she meant the crayons, and so did the little girl sitting beside me. We were on our way out of the classroom together when the teacher grabbed us and turned us round. 'That's stealing!' she said, and took the boxes of crayons from us. She had only meant us to take the drawings, and she wouldn't listen to us, wouldn't believe we had misunderstood. She made us cross our hands in turn, and she belted us. Tears came to my eyes from the pain and from helpless, impotent rage. I ran home, still crying. I had wet myself. My mother was there to comfort and calm me, but neither of my parents seemed to understand the full horror. In fact they were sending me back to school next day! That monster of a woman had beaten me, for nothing, and they were sending me back to her! Then began the slow painful process, the loss of implicit faith in my parents. The teacher, and the school, had a power, and my parents could do nothing against it.

Things were never quite the same after that. Something had changed in me, hardened. But then it was never really quite so

17

bad again as in those first few weeks. This new reality that had seemed so alien and hostile, this too was becoming everyday and normal. But never ever did I come to love it. Weekends and holidays were precious.

The earliest holiday I remember was for the Coronation. Every child received a tin of sweets with the Queen's portrait on the lid. I went with my mother to visit my aunt, one of the first people in the area, perhaps in the whole of Glasgow, to have a television set. The set was tiny, with a nine-inch screen, and the house was full of neighbours, crowding round to watch. Afterwards, in the back court, somebody gave a party for all the local children, with crisps and ice-lollies and paper hats, party-games and songs and jokes. It was a great, great day. God save the Queen!

The Queen was a Protestant. My uncle had told me that. My uncle was in the Orange Lodge, and had undertaken my education in such matters. He and my father had already taken me to see Rangers play at Ibrox. I had felt the elation at their victory, the depression at their defeat; I had been initiated. Emotionally now I could feel the connections; the Queen and the Union Jack, being a Protestant and following Rangers; it was all noble and good, all part of some glorious heritage that was mine. And the opposite of all this was Catholic, was darkness, was bad and in some way a threat.

I remember one day my uncle teaching me about colours. I was wearing a blue jersey and he said it was good, was a fine colour.

How about orange, I asked, was that a good colour? The best, he said.

Purple? That was good too.

Red was fine.

Black and white were OK, not good, not bad.

But green was bad. The worst.

I thought of the green park where we went on those summer evenings, and how beautiful it was. But no. It was the colour of Celtic, of the Catholics. They had made it their own, had made it bad.

I was eating further of the tree of knowledge.

My uncle said I was growing into a good Protestant. He said when I was a little older he would get me into the Juvenile Orange Lodge. The thought excited me.

I could march in a parade, perhaps even learn to play flute or drum in a band. But my mother said no. They were all mad she said, just making people hate each other all the more, and for nothing.

Reality was growing more complex and confusing. Nothing, it seemed, was clear cut.

At school I was making progress. That ogre of a teacher was replaced by another, much milder, and I began to flower. From the age of six on, through my whole time at the school, I came top in every exam, won first prize every year. Teachers made much of me. My drawings and my handwriting were often on display. I was granted little privileges, like being sent on errands, minutes of glorious freedom from the class. I developed a certain smugness, a pride in my own abilities, a sense that I was special, unique. And to those teachers I suppose I was. Ours was one of the rougher schools in a rough part of the city.

Unemployment was high, there was real poverty, and much small-scale crime. The school itself had some reputation—it was overcrowded, and many of the children were 'problem-cases'.

To the teachers, my little bright spark of intelligence would be something that had to be nurtured and encouraged to grow. One teacher in particular had great hopes for me. She suggested that when I reached the right age, I should try the scholarship exam for a high school in the city centre. The school was fee-paying, but a small number of bursaries were awarded each year, on the basis of a competitive exam. This teacher encouraged me to read more widely, sometimes gave me extra work, to prepare me. I liked her better than any of the other teachers.

One morning, I was about eight at the time, she came in raging and started to rant at us about the prime minister, Anthony Eden. He had sent bombers to Suez, she said, while at the same time the British government was condemning Russia for invading Hungary. We listened, amazed. These were things we had heard about from the world of the newspapers, of the radio, but it was all beyond our comprehension. And here was our teacher, turning on its head the way we had come to see things, where the British, which was us, were always in the right. Reality was becoming complex indeed. There was a whole big world out there, full of contradictions.

And how did I fit into it? How was my definition of myself shaping up? Well, I was a Protestant, I knew that. I also knew that I was Scottish. Scotland was my country, Glasgow my city. Sometimes being Scottish meant being British, sometimes British just

19

meant English. But then sometimes Scottish and English were opposed, as in football internationals, as in great battles from the past. My idea of what British meant came originally from war films I had seen. British were soldiers who wore a certain shape of helmet. The other kinds were Americans, Germans and Japs. British and Americans were always good, the others were bad. But in Korean War films, the Americans were fighting communists, and my father had said my teacher was a communist. It was all too confusing.

About this time too I joined the Lifeboys and started going to Sunday-school. The Lifeboys were Protestant, connected with the Church of Scotland, but they didn't offend my mother the way the Orange Lodge did. The Lifeboys would be a good healthy influence.

The Lifeboys met in a church hall once a week. We played games and did a lot of marching. After a few months I made it into the football team, at outside-right. That was a great delight to me, since our school didn't have a team and there was no other way I could play in one. In those days nothing made me happier than football, watching it, reading about it, and most of all playing it. I was small and thin, not well able to withstand crunching tackles. But I could run fast and pass the ball well, skills that kept me out of trouble and carried me through.

In the same church where the Lifeboys met, I started going to the Sunday morning services, after which we met for Sunday school. I don't remember much about those sessions, just a grey interminable boredom. There seemed to be endless dull talk. The minister and the elders all seemed dour. The Sunday school teachers, though young, had all prematurely stiffened into the attitudes and mannerisms of middle-age.

The little I knew of the Catholic church seemed much more attractive, perhaps all the more so for being forbidden. They had statues and images, rosaries and medallions and holy pictures. They had the mysterious ceremony of the Mass, they had chanting and singing, and, most beautiful of all, they worshipped Mary, Our Lady, God as a woman. The Catholic church seemed feminine and bright. The Church of Scotland seemed stern and upright and grim. (I also had a secret and hopeless love for a little Catholic girl, which may have contributed to the picture!)

If it had been possible, I would have gone to the Catholic church. But I couldn't even voice such a thought. It would have

20

been heresy. So instead I changed from the big church to a small mission-hall, the Glasgow City Mission. Here there was much less talk and more singing. The people seemed relaxed, the atmosphere generally oppressive.

In charge of the Mission was a tiny wee man who was fired with a frantic kind of energy. He was never happier than when leading us all in song, conducting us as if we were some vast choir. My father called him 'Heavenly Sunshine', because that was the wee man's favourite hymn.

'Heavenly Sunshine
Heavenly Sunshine
Flooding my soul with
Glory Divine . . .'

I was happy at the Mission the way I had never been at the church; and I could still go to the Lifeboys, still had my precious football. For a time I was very pious, felt a pure light within me. I started to read a little New Testament I had been given. I went to the Mission two or three nights a week, for Bible Class, Band of Hope, anything and everything.

But at times there was another side to me, a side that would have smashed all this, that hated being the good boy, hated school and its stupid values, hated all confinement and constraint. And I would go rampaging with a gang of friends, yelling, fighting, swearing, vandalising. Then I would feel penitent, go through inner agonies and turmoil; and at last that pure flame would rekindle inside me. I had not, after all, been forsaken and damned.

Meanwhile at school, I was still 'doing well'. My parents and relatives were proud of me, sure that I was going to 'get on'.

I remember my auntie telling me to stick in and get myself a good job. 'Collar an' tie,' she said. 'Never have tae take yer jacket off.'

Every year the local paper, the *Govan Press*, printed a list of school prizewinners. Every year my mother cut out the list, and she kept the cuttings pressed in a book. My father could already see me going on to University, becoming a doctor or a lawyer. What I wanted was to be an artist, or perhaps a writer. Drawing and painting were what I liked best, and writing compositions (next, of course, to football, and I knew already I wasn't good enough ever to make the grade at that).

One day we had to write a composition on 'What I want to be.'

I wrote that I wanted to be an artist, and my teacher told me not to be so stupid.

I was eleven then, and the bursary exam was coming up within the year. I was made to feel it was tremendously important. There was a pressure on me to pass. Then something happened that cut across all my little concerns, turned my whole world upside down.

My mother had been ill, on and off, for as long as I could remember, with that same recurring asthma and bronchitis. In between times she was back working at the bakery. Her illness was simply a fact of life, one that we had grown used to. A change of air would have helped her. To give up working would have helped her. But these things were impossible. She died in the Southern General Hospital late one Sunday night, thirty-eight years old.

I was numbed by the grief and pain of it, the first pain of loss. But nothing really changed. The world went on, regardless. The first sharp pain of it would ease, but a deep, deep ache would linger.

There was something else too that would linger, something I have tried before to put into words. On the day of my mother's funeral, there was suddenly this feeling; I knew that there was something more than this sadness, something behind and beyond it. My physical mother was dead, but her love for me, mother-love itself, was all-pervading. I could feel it, in the soft wind that blew, touching everything. It was intimately connected with Our Lady, the Mother of God, whose blue robes I could see in the blue of the sky. I had glimpsed an aspect of the divine mother, and in later years I was to remember it often, and to understand in part what was meant by resurrection.

When I went back to school I felt older, I felt changed. In a sense my childhood was over. The first throes of adolescence would be on me soon enough. And another time-cycle was also over. It was 1959; the fifties were drawing to a close. With my father, I watched a television programme that looked back over the decade. They showed film-clips of the Coronation, of Churchill and Eisenhower and Eden; of Korea and Suez and Hungary; of the first Sputnik; they showed changing fashions in clothes and cars; they showed teddy-boys and rock-and-roll riots, Bill Haley and Little Richard and Elvis Presley; they showed an old man shaking his head at it and asking if it was for this we had won the war.

For me, the new decade brought its changes early. It was soon time to sit the bursary exam. When the day came I was terrified.

22

So much had been put on the exam for so long. I went, dickied up in my Sunday suit, a shirt and tie, shiny black shoes. There were five hundred entrants competing for some thirty or forty places.

The paper was in two parts, English and Arithmetic. The English I coasted, dashed off the Interpretation, wrote a happy composition about 'My Hobby', which at that time was collecting football programmes. In the Arithmetic paper I became bogged down, went too slowly, didn't answer all the questions. There were too many problems that were unfamiliar to me, too many tricks I didn't know. It was a disaster. The long bus-journey home was desolation. I told everyone who asked that I had failed. I sat in the toilet and cried till I was dry-eyed. Then I resigned myself to it. I would be happier at the local high school, not separated from my friends. I changed into my old clothes and sandshoes. I went out into the back court and kicked a ball against the wall for a long, long time.

A few weeks later, a fat letter arrived telling me I had passed. I couldn't believe it. My father was jubilant, my teachers proud. I had done it. I was on my way.

Somehow my father managed, probably by borrowing, to kit me out with the school uniform—navy blue blazer with the school badge, grey trousers, a striped tie and a cap. I felt stiff and awkward in it, but the wearing of it was compulsory.

Once more I had to adapt to a new set of constraints, restrictions, disciplines. In the new school, the day was divided up into forty-minute periods. Bells summoned us from one to the next. We had to find our way around the school's rambling corridors, its four floors, its annexes. We were not allowed to leave the school at lunchtime, for fear we might be knocked down in the city-centre traffic. In those first days I was spun and buffeted in yet another strange new world that both attracted and repelled me. I had been pitched from a little local primary school into this institution, so conscious of its own tradition and heritage. I was made to feel that I had taken a step up on the ladder. There were hundreds of boys (no girls), all presumably drawn from the best pupils in schools all over the city. For the first time I encountered boys from another social class, noticed a general confident assurance, a level of articulation I had never met before.

I felt there were new universes opening up to me. There was much to learn; there was an allure in the names of completely new subjects—Physics and Chemistry, Geometry and Algebra and Latin.

But I found the general atmosphere of rigour oppressive. As in the primary school, there were teachers who saw their first task as breaking our spirit, imposing their own will. We were there to learn, and they would make sure we did. There was the physics teacher who belted anyone who carelessly botched an experiment. There was the music teacher who belted half the class for not sight-reading well enough. There was the geography teacher who gave out lines by the hundred if you couldn't churn out the names of rivers or ports or capital cities on demand. Perhaps most telling of all, there was the Latin teacher who belted all those who couldn't conjugate the verb *amare*—to love. Young though I was, I could see the irony in that!

But of course there were others; a mild and kindly English teacher, an art teacher who was flamboyant and expansive, a chemistry teacher with a manic sense of humour, and many more, just ordinary decent men, coping with a difficult job. It was simply a matter of luck which teachers you happened to be assigned to, and how that coloured your first impressions of a subject. For my part, I worked hard at the subjects I liked, made a truce with those I hated, and muddled along in the rest.

At the end of my first year, I came out top in English, Latin and Art. I did fairly well in the science subjects, less well in Maths and Geography, and very badly in the practical workshop studies —woodwork and metalwork.

My interests and abilities, then, lay a little to one side of the mainstream. For the emphasis in the school was very firmly on the science side. The founder had been a well-known engineer and industrialist, and the school had always prided itself in contributing to a great Scottish tradition in the number of scientists and engineers it had produced. The arts subjects were definitely regarded as peripheral.

In a year or two I would have to choose, in fact, between art and science, a choice that would shape the course of future studies. But for now I had other concerns. Many things were changing and breaking up around me.

Already I was losing contact with my old friends from Govan. We were apart during the day at our different schools, and often enough in the evenings I would have homework to keep me in. A gradual gulf opened up.

I had also grown too old for the Sunday school and the Lifeboys. It was time to graduate to the church and the Boys' Brigade. I gave the Church of Scotland another try and still found it pompous and serious. It made me uncomfortable. In the Boys Brigade too, the same stuffy spirit seemed to prevail. They were trying too hard to make decent Christian men of us. There was quite enough dryness at school for one young life, and I left both the church and the B.B. The one thing I regretted was giving up the chance of playing in a football team. For our school played rugby, ostensibly because it allowed more people to play, but really, I was sure, out of class-consciousness. Football was for scruffs and rugby was a cut above it. I went once to rugby practice. I was heavily tackled and pounded into the ground, I twisted a knee, in a scrum I was butted in the chin and bit my tongue. And that was enough.

At home we began clearing out the room so that I could have it for my own and not have to go on sharing the kitchen with my father. It was good to have my own space. I defined it as mine by putting pictures on the wall—a coloured photo of Rangers, a picture cut from a newspaper of cosmonaut Yuri Gagarin who had just circled the world in the first manned space-flight.

Looking back on it, I can see that wall as an ever-changing map of the various stages I went through, where I recorded each new definition of myself. The next few years saw many such changes.

The onset of puberty, of course, brought its turmoil and its anguish, awakening to my own sexuality, unfulfillable yearning, delight of masturbation and the terrible guilty secret of it. Since leaving primary school I had already grown shy of girls, and being at an all-boys school intensified it.

It was a lonely time, out of touch with old friends, never seeing any new friends outside of school, since they lived too far away. There was a stage when I grew nervous and morose, often cried for no reason. I retreated more and more into the comfort and refuge of a fantasy-world, of books, of pop music from the radio.

Reason and doubt too were developing. I had lost the simple faith of my earlier years. Sweet Jesus, and even Mother Mary, meant little to me. God was the stern father of the Old Testament, the grim righteousness of the kirk, something to be feared, and rejected.

New pictures went up on my wall; girl singers and actresses, Susan Maughan and Hayley Mills; rock-and-roll bands, the Shadows, the Tornadoes.

Often life was unbearably serious! I remember during the Cuban missile crisis I was sure the war was on us at last. I stayed away from school, wallowing a little in despair. I went walking in the park, quietly preparing myself for the end. But it didn't end. Things went on as before. I was almost disappointed. There was another stage when I became obsessed, still in a very romantic way, with Russia and China and the idea of revolution. I became aware of the inadequacies of our own social system. (From Govan they were not hard to see.) And up on my wall went Lenin and Marx.

Through all these changes, I had one close friend. We both did well at our schoolwork, picked up prizes every year. But we felt stifled by the outer constraints that the school imposed. The living image of all that we hated and feared was the headmaster. Black-cloaked, he would swoop round the school, stilling an unruly queue by his very presence, pulling people up for being rowdy, or untidy, or showing some slight discrepancy in their uniform—brown shoes instead of black, no cap, the wrong colour of pullover. He would frequently lecture classes, or sometimes the whole school, on some aspect of discipline. To the pupils he was known simply as 'The Boss'.

I can see now that the man had a certain dignity, stood by standards he had to uphold. He once moved me deeply, on the morning after President Kennedy's assassination, when he made a speech to the whole school, saying what he felt about it. 'Take care in your own lives,' he said, 'lest you murder not men but principles.'

But from where we stood then, 'The Boss' had to be fought.

As early as first year, my friend and I decided we would one day be beatniks. Another time we called ourselves pagans, and at yet another stage, we wanted to become Druids, which we decided was our true religion. In all this was a strange prefiguring of changes we would go through in later years, in the late sixties, when we would become drop-outs, call ourselves 'hippies', search for meaning in any and every religious tradition, and in none. But all that was still to come.

Our schooldays spanned the years when rock music was becoming a force, an influence on a whole generation. The Beatles and the Rolling Stones went up on my wall. So did the young Bob Dylan. We wanted, now simultaneously, now alternately, to be mods and rockers. We were learning about our world, not from school, but from television and radio, records and films.

At school we had a running battle with the headmaster. We cultivated scruffiness, wore coloured shirts and waistcoats, grew

26

our hair long. A strange flowering in grey Glasgow. The head-master gave us lines, belted us, threatened us with expulsion. We played a strange kind of hide-and-seek, keeping out of his way. The Who were singing about 'My Generation'.

> 'People try to p-put us down
> J-just because we g-get around
> Things they do look awful cold
> Hope I die before I get old!'

And yet in all our bravado, there was a certain paradoxical in-nocence, for we were still doing our schoolwork, passing our ex-ams, collecting prizes; we were still, at one level, being good little boys, still following a well-marked route towards jobs, success, respectability.

At the end of fifth year we took our Highers, next step in the rung. My friend decided to leave then and get a job. I stayed on for a sixth year in a state of total confusion about my future. Swayed by some sense of 'practicality', I had taken science in-stead of art, but I didn't want to go on studying it. What I really wanted now was to be a writer, and I knew no course of study could lead me to that. I had started writing poetry, after reading Dylan Thomas. My first poems were about Govan, the environment I knew and my childhood there.

During the free space I had in sixth year, I read more poetry. I discovered Allen Ginsberg and the other American Beat poets. Freedom was beckoning. I still kept contact with my friend. He had a regular girlfriend now and was talking of getting married. I had lost my tortured shyness of girls, but retained a certain awe of them that had me writing abysmally bad love-poems. Then, led on by the influence of the Beat poets, I began to read a little about Eastern religions. And I felt for what I read a joyful recognition.

Down came all the pictures from my wall, and instead I drew with a felt-tip pen, directly on to the wall, a life-size seated figure of the Buddha.

And this was an early sign of the direction I was to move in, towards an inner search. It was 1966. Within a year or two my friend and I had both dropped out, he from his job and I from university. We set off on a journey to London, moving out from the narrow confines of childhood and adolescence.

We would have to break and throw aside all those values we had received, if only to rediscover them for ourselves.

27

Much was still to be broken down in us. The journey we had started on was to lead us in separate ways, forever moving towards our own fulfilment, towards knowing who we are. I was to open myself once more to that gentle presence I had known as a child. In moving towards a new wholeness, I was to see the fragmentation of those years as just stages in a process, an endless process of becoming.

CATHERINE CZERKAWSKA

A Sheltered Wilderness

Sometimes I pretend that I'm Scottish, but I'm not really. I was born in Leeds. Later, we moved to London and then, in 1963, on to Scotland, where my parents settled in Ayrshire: 'The Burns Country'. The tourist brochures said that it was beautiful. I knew nothing about it except that at the time, I didn't want to go.

On my mother's side, my grandfather was a big Viking of York-shire Dales stock, a family washed up on the tide of the Industrial Revolution and left strained in smoky, sprawling Leeds. My grand-mother was Irish: a brisk, loving, well-upholstered lady. My mother, their youngest daughter, was a beautiful Yorkshire girl with a wicked sense of humour, who did the daring thing and married a foreigner. My father's family were Polish aristocrats—extrovert and charming. A thread of something rich, strange and superbly foreign ran through my childhood.

I was a shy, only child when we arrived in Scotland—a loner but rarely lonely. I had grown up with my own company and liked it well enough. The first thing I saw on our arrival was the sea. It consoled me. To live 'at the seaside' is a daydream of so many city children. 'It'll put some roses back in your cheeks,' said my mother. Half my early years had been spent grappling with bouts of asthma. I was pale, but I had never been allowed the indulgence of looking frail. 'Surely you're as strong as a horse,' people would say. I was always robust. Now, I suddenly found that I needed to be.

My new school was a bombshell. It was a rough, tough, Roman Catholic comprehensive. Everyone went there, although we were streamed into three classes—bright, indifferent and hopeless. I came straight from a disciplined, acutely civilised convent grammar school, where girls called Penelope and Deborah pattered down highly polished corridors in smart blue uniforms; where everyone had a crush on the drama teacher; where all the youngsters covertly admired the pretty sixth formers who pinned their school hats to the backs of their curly or smooth heads with such chic. Now, here I was, with my rather broad vowels, my different vocabulary and all the physical awkwardness of adolescence, lost in a wilderness, And what's more, a wilderness containing Boys. My fellow pupils' suspicion of me was palpable and my own tongue-tied inadequacy linked up with that hostility to form a vicious circle which made my first few years there a torment. 'Settling down' was a long and painful process, only truly accomplished when, at the age of sixteen, we all moved to another school to complete our fifth and sixth years.

Initially, though, my life assumed a dual character along a school/home axis. No weekend passes now, without my thanking heaven that I no longer need suffer from that Sunday night sinking feeling which haunted my childhood. Nor do I ever smell the stale gymshoe aroma of classrooms without flinching a little.

It was at this time that I began to write in earnest—partly to escape from uncongenial surroundings, but more urgently, out of a desperate need to communicate. I needed somehow to externalise the half-formed feelings and ideas which I was far too shy to discuss openly. Consequently, I was rarely reluctant to show those first raw poems to other people. I wanted them to be seen. Bad as they were, they at least spoke where I could not. They were a plea for understanding which I suspect is common to many writers. The writer, no matter how amateur, is always greedy for love.

It seems to me sometimes that my experiences at school, even divided my apprehension of Scotland into two distinct parts. One is always associated with all those things that meant school, and school in turn meant the everyday Scotland of haggis suppers and scruffy anoraks, Glasgow comedians and fried dumpling, afternoon teas and football and graffiti. That was how I saw it then, and that is how it still strikes me sometimes—often with that pleasant familiarity which amounts to deep affection, occasionally with a great pang of irritation. It was a very foreign place. Home was simply another and more familiar country.

I had always possessed the ability to hedge myself in with fantasy and for the first few years I never allowed school to become very real for me. Later, I fell in love—a sort of schoolgirl equivalent of courtly love, endured but never consummated—and the infrequent glimpses of the beloved were incentive enough. I rarely woke up wanting to go to school, but I was fairly happy.

I can remember a feeling of resignation. My education had to be got through. I knew that things could only get better. Meanwhile, my imagination was a shield.

There were some things, however, which touched me more closely. School had its sordid aspects. Two youths had burned down the main building a short time before my arrival and conditions were far from ideal. The burning seemed to have had a depressing effect on the morale of the whole school. But the most objectionable and shocking thing from my point of view was the excessive and indiscriminate use of corporal punishment—'the belt'—that archaic strip of leather which did nothing but harden hands and hearts. There was an element of sadism in it all, which I even then recognised; which is probably still present. The belt was rarely used 'in moderation' at my school. There was something degrading about the twisted mouths of the men cold-bloodedly wielding this medieval implement; or the idiotic bouncing figures of the semi-hysterical women who belted every day for work unlearnt, for lateness, for talking. And there was something degrading too in the most frequent victim's defiant grin or in our, the audience's, unwilling excitement. There was a peculiar attraction and a terrible savagery in it, the memory of which is very distasteful. But at the same time the rule of misdemeanour and subsequent violent punishment had become so fixed that the whole exercise became a dreary and pointless ritual. In all my years at school I can never remember anybody being really deterred from doing anything by the threat of a belting.

I had never experienced violence of this kind before. Suddenly, I became aware of barriers between myself and the adults I had been so free with. Perhaps this is why, in many cases, the teaching itself had become a joyless process with teachers unable to communicate a pleasure in study they had long since lost. Even when they had retained some essential spark our own minds were often irrevocably closed by the convention of hostility between teacher and pupil. Learning was not to be enjoyed. It was considered odd to study, peculiar to be interested, strange to do your work well. You never answered in class without being prompted. You never said anything at all if you could possibly help it.

To be fair, the system suited me well enough. At my old convent school the competitive academic pressure had been tremendous. Once that pressure was lifted I felt free to explore in my own sweet way and my learning certainly didn't suffer. At that age, anything which stretches the mind suffices—always providing that you have enough encouragement in the home, and a good grounding in most subjects. I was lucky. It certainly lightened my heart to see my mathematician father sweating and cursing, trying to explain arithmetic problems ('Why the hell would six men want to fill an eight-foot bath in three hours?') which we both realised that neither of us could do. But then my father was a very subversive influence. 'You'd be using calculators for stuff like this anyway,' he would hiss, and instead, he would fill my head full of fascinating mathematical paradoxes and stories of flatlanders and moebus strips!

The system at that time was basically effective, but lacking in imagination. Pupils were given as much factual general knowledge about as many subjects as possible. Education must be seen to be effective and you frequently heard, 'He/she's quite brilliant; got five Highers.' But when you realised that, in order to pass SCE Higher French at that time, you needn't even have read a full-length novel in the language, the achievement became less impressive. Students were not encouraged to think for themselves, and largely did not want to. There was an uneasy feeling current that this might be construed as questioning the traditional, received knowledge, and education was nothing if not hierarchical. My really valuable learning was done alone, with the encouragement of my parents, or during my last years at school, where I came into contact with several capable teachers.

People influence us by our dislike of them as much as by our respect for them. So many subjects were made boring by boring exponents or frightening by impatient ones. There were, nevertheless, at least a few teachers for whom one could claim a real fondness. One was a Latin teacher with a long sad face and a dry sense of humour, who treated his classes very much as people and woefully crammed Latin grammar into us while somehow managing to show us something of the satisfaction of logic. The other was an angry, temperamental but essentially kindhearted music teacher who insisted on nothing less than perfection and persuaded us that if he believed in our capabilities we could produce minor miracles. Our choral singing that year won prizes, but it was mostly due to our rapport with him. He gave us a tremendous sense of loyalty and gained my undying affection by allowing me to practice for piano exams in the school hall whenever I could manage to get out of P.T. lessons.

32

Scottish schools, like their English counterparts, have an unhealthy preoccupation with physical fitness. But in my first Scots school this was coupled with a real mistrust of art and things artistic. Such things could hardly be counted as work. Work, like education, is, by definition, unpleasant. Strenuous if possible. P.T. therefore was fine, although painting was not. I remember with exultation the day one fresh-faced lady in her navy blue divided skirt ordered us to leap from a springboard to a box to a trampoline to a horse at full height, and was flattened by the first over-enthusiastic pupil to come sailing over.

Religion also loomed very large. We read books about the Bible (rather than the Bible itself—we were supposed to do that on our own initiative) and had daring discussions. It was still a mortal sin to miss Mass on Sunday, meaning that if you didn't go and then you died, you went straight to hell. But I think we compromised on that one. Occasionally, a priest came to see us, especially a young endearing soul who threw chalk at talkers and rode a wild motorbike. At my second Scottish school, a mixed convent school, one of the sisters explained to our class of sixteen-year-olds how we mustn't indulge in kissing until we were engaged because it might lead to 'other things'. We knew, we knew.

Mixed schools are a mixed blessing. In an ideal situation they ought to mean that boys and girls grow up in a simple comradely atmosphere and pay more attention to their work than they otherwise might. But we were only human and the teenage years were fraught with far more distractions than one could possibly experience at single-sex schools. Sex, after all, is a pretty distracting thing normally, and even more so in an academic desert. (I suppose that's why it's such a popular university pastime.) We were not immune. One needs some relief from 'O' Levels. Also we, the girls, felt separate, forced into extremes of femininity by the very presence of boys, and not perhaps as free in our academic choices as we might have been. I expect that the same applied to the boys. In some subjects, e.g. Domestic Science or Woodwork, the school inhibited us. But then most of us had never dreamed that girls could do such patently masculine work. Neither we nor our parents queried the status quo and often we simply inhibited ourselves. Equality was only a vague idea filtering through. I suspect that even now it has little support in most Scottish secondary schools. I remember the son of a friend being laughed to scorn for his desire to learn cookery instead of technical drawing. In

33

many ways I was lucky. As an only child I had fulfilled the functions of both a son and a daughter and consequently I was ready to tackle most things. As it turned out my natural favourites were the 'feminine' Arts subjects but I certainly passed my pre-adolescent years as a tomboy who swarmed up walls and took to the woods occasionally wearing a Davy Crockett hat and carrying a rifle.

In our early teenage it was not our classmates who appealed to us: not the 'clever' boys who seemed to be so emotionally and physically immature. But the C classes with their cave-man appeal attracted us enormously. Many of them were big tough boys, raring to get away from school and into a job. They scorned uniform and slouched around in jeans. Their hands were horny from frequent strappings and they were afraid of nobody. Often their home backgrounds were unhappy; most of them had been deprived of books, if nothing else.

In my fourth year I was a prefect. Leon was a big, blue-eyed, black-haired Irish-Scots ruffian, who led a gang of boys on forays every lunchtime. It was a primitive and enchanting game. They pestered us, using all possible strategies to get into the school building. We—the girls—threw them out with maddening insistence. But they were bigger and stronger than us. The encounters frequently erupted into delicious physical contact with just the right threat of violence. Leon never let things get out of hand. Nobody got hurt. Like so many of those boys he was a clever troublemaker who infuriated his male teachers and left them frustrated and angry. But there was no real malice in him and memories of him live on to substantiate the female fantasy of the rough diamond. Or perhaps it's just that no judgement of anyone can ever be final; no one can ever see the whole picture.

Later, we became more sophisticated in our tastes, or so we thought: went to parties where we drank cheap wine and played Postman's Knock, fixing the numbers, giving and receiving chaste, wet passionless kisses outside the door, or danced smoochily to Jim Reeves and the Beatles. The Beatles pursued us through our teens. John Lennon was my great idol. I sat through 'A Hard Day's Night' and 'Help' repeatedly; changed my allegiance from John to Ringo and knew all the words of all the songs, a fact which now severely dates both myself and my friends.

The parties were a disappointment. The gap between fantasy and reality was too wide for me really to enjoy myself and like

34

the Postman's Knock kisses, there was always that inexplicable feeling of let-down afterwards. Sex was all-pervasive at that time, although we did not admit it blatantly. We felt a certain amount of guilt. We were at the awkward age; certainly not honest enough to say, as one friend later so ruefully remarked, 'You know, almost all my thoughts are dirty.'

The boys told rude jokes during rainy lunchtimes. Someone brought *The Carpetbaggers* to school and we read the relevant grubby pages with avid curiosity. One girl had heard her parents making love in the next room. With all the narrow-minded arrogance of youth, we were shocked right through to our Marks and Sparks knickers. I had a crush on a tall blond boy who wore a long fringe, cuban-heeled boots and black-rimmed spectacles, following the fashion of the time. He was clever and popular and he never gave me a second glance. But then I hardly expected it. I fell in love—genuine, ghastly, first love—a little later with the boy who was to marry one of my best friends. It was my one and only experience of love at first sight and it was utterly shattering. The crisis came several months later, at the big event of the year—the senior dance.

We talked about those dances for weeks beforehand, planning dresses and make-up; speculating as to who liked whom. One month before, the P.T. fiends donned their dancing shoes, herded us into the gym, forced the reluctant boys to take random partners, more often than not much taller than themselves, and tried to teach us civilised dances, like foxtrots and waltzes and the Gay Gordons. Eightsome Reels were the worst and always ended in utter chaos with boys setting gingerly to other boys and Mr Blank in his tracksuit bellowing directions and manipulating Jimmy Shand on the rickety gramophone.

The dances themselves were held in the school hall under the gory traditional statue of Christ on the Crucifix. The nuns came to watch us enjoy ourselves and to monitor the pointedness of our heels. 'That dress doesn't really suit you, Catherine,' said one of them sweetly. Some of the boys had been drinking. The smell of peppermints was overpowering as we stumbled around the polished parquet floors.

At that particular dance all those first and worst agonies of unrequited love seemed to be focused on me. I felt like the only soul left on earth with everyone else in paradise. In the grubby, slogan-scrawled station waiting-room on the way home, the black-

35

ness in my head alarmed me. 'Do you know,' said one of the boys, looking at the back-to-front reflections on the window of the train, 'that Troon is Noort, backwards.' I wondered how I could even hear anyone talking through all the misery.

Later, we went to other, less innocent dances at the crumbling Pavilion, down by the seashore and I was consoled by a gentle brush salesman with a wolfish face—another ruffian—who kissed me tenderly in the rain. Nothing had ever felt so good. He wanted to take me home in his big green van but I wouldn't let him. I was sixteen and scared as much of myself as of him. It was all touch and then go as far as most of us were concerned.

Meanwhile, in the solitude of home, I read indiscriminately and avidly. Books had always been part and parcel of my childhood. Now I graduated to D. H. Lawrence, Tolkien, Dylan Thomas and the book every romantic novelist wishes she had written—*Wuthering Heights*—parts of which I knew by heart. I read Ibsen's *Peer Gynt* while I was still in my early teens, only half-understood it, and found myself two suitably depressive Norwegian penfriends. 'Last night I roll in snow in my pyjamas and look at sky,' wrote one, dramatically. The other arrived, long and alarming, with a big Mary Poppins umbrella and a rucksack. I was terrified lest suburban Ayrshire should see us together and fobbed him off on my parents for most of the weekend.

From reluctantly reciting 'To a Mouse' at school, I discovered Robert Burns' love poetry and began to be interested. I went on Saturday pilgrimages to the little stone cottage where he was born and lurked in the darkest corners waiting for a ghost which stubbornly refused to materialise. Even in winter when the place was empty of tourists I didn't hear so much as a hollow moan. However, I never lost heart, but wandered along ye banks and braes o' bonnie Doon (and there are none bonnier) or into the eerie churchyard where Tam o' Shanter had the temerity to yell out 'Weel done, cutty sark!' (Well done, short shirt!) to the most attractive member of a coven of witches, and just escaped with his life but left his horse's tail behind him. Seances with a tumbler and little bits of paper were a dismal failure, but even so, this total absorption in a landscape, and with a body of literature gave me a sharp awareness of atmosphere—a sense of place which I have vainly tried to recapture since. It is a thing of adolescence and is later glimpsed only briefly; never with that first heartbreaking clarity. We gather emotional skins until our hides are tough as trees.

36

The Ayrshire landscape had taken a fierce hold on me. My parents and I spent a lot of time in the countryside during those years and eventually lived there. Later summer was the best time with the sloping fields and corn stooks sharply defined by shadows, house martins clustering to set off south and disturbing, doomsday, blood-red sunsets behind the Isle of Arran. Never before or since has a landscape seethed with so many conjured phantoms for me. The place was enchanted. The lonely hills and moorlands were full of Celts in gold and leather—like the princes of Aeron who fought for the Eastern kingdom of Goddodin against the Saxons and returned. They were the lucky ones.

'There were three hundred, three score and three gold torqued warriors' the poem says. 'But after all the flowing mead, from those that went to war, only three by bravery in battle escaped— Aeron's two war hounds and brave Cynon.'

The kingdom of Goddodin, with its capital where Edinburgh now stands, was extensive and rich. But the Saxons were gaining in strength. The warriors went on a customary pre-battle drinking bout and were slaughtered by their stronger foes. The two young men from Ayrshire escaped. I found myself wondering who watched for them, with what delighted incredulity from what hill-top fortress?

I absorbed a hellish brew of Arthurian Mythology and the Golden Bough. It didn't seem to do me any harm. I ransacked the library for old histories and nineteenth century archaeological reports of the area, written by ubiquitous, bicycle-equipped clergymen, inaccurate and readable. Then we went on hilarious weekend expeditions in search of ancient monuments where people fell in streams and my marvellous happy-go-lucky mother dried them out, sliced bread, fried frozen steaks in the rain and always forgot the sugar. Sawney Bean and his family lurked below Bennane Head, still waiting to cannibalise unwary travellers as they had done so many hundreds of years before. The southern hills were full of gypsies who at any moment might carry you off to a lonely cave. The wild Kennedy family had once inhabited a string of fortresses along the coast. They fought each other savagely, but united against all opposition. In my imagination, I heard the thunder of their hooves over old stone bridges, or the cries of the Abbot of Crossraguel being roasted in Dunure Castle—one of the less subtle forms of blackmail employed by the owner, a Kennedy, who wanted the rich Abbey lands signed over into his keeping.

Much to my appreciation, we moved into a house which possessed a real ghost. We had a flat in the oldest part of what had once been a coaching inn. A tall man in a brown cloak walked quickly past the kitchen window at intervals. I kept quiet about it until I found my mother looking suspiciously behind a rhododendron bush one day. 'I could have sworn I saw somebody round here,' she said. The dog watched things that nobody else could see, glassy eyed. But he was a nice old ghost and frightened nobody— a bright, sunlit ghost who came only on hot summer afternoons.

Most of my friends were planning to go to Glasgow University or teacher training college and travel home at weekends. I wanted to go farther afield but I was still not ready to leave the shelter that Scotland had become. Edinburgh seemed, to a seventeen-year-old, to possess the required measure of glamour, apart from which it was, quite simply, a beautiful city. I was scared out of my wits at the idea of leaving home but we all knew that I had better make the break. And that made it easier. On our last school speech day I cried, as did so many of my friends, because we realised, in the panic of parting, the depths of our affection for each other, for many of our teachers, and for the school. How safe and secure the classrooms seemed!

Edinburgh lived up to expectations. If my move there did not exactly signify the end of childhood it was certainly the beginning of the end—the end of Scotland as my all in all. Edinburgh was full of intimations of another, wider world which I badly wanted to see. The grass isn't always greener on the other side of the fence but the different varieties are well worth inspection.

What I lacked then and still lack, is the mature regard which belongs to the place or person where or with whom one finally settles down—a certain contentment which I have not yet achieved. Nor, I have to admit, will I ever feel Scottish as I feel English in Yorkshire or Polish in Warsaw. That's something different again—a gut reaction, like family feeling. Now, with half my belongings on opposite sides of Europe, I am still looking for something I may well discover on my own doorstep, because I still find myself defending Scotland with a fierce loyalty when I am away, still remembering places, people, times with the occasional pang of homesickness, still coming back only to leave again. Maybe I'll never really be a Scottish writer: simply a writer with, among other things, a Scottish childhood.

MARTIN MACDONALD

John Equals Ian QED

Late Friday afternoon in early summer is not the best of times to lead civil servants down the more abstruse byways of Gaelic etymology. So that Friday afternoon of May 1960, in a fourth-floor office in one of the tall crescents off the West End of Edinburgh, I was having trouble with my civil servant. He was as nondescript as a civil servant ought to be; smallish; vaguely middle-aged; skimpy, sandy hair; the impression of a brown suit. And he was obviously prepared to allow the irritability that was his habit of office flower into full-blown exasperation.

His problem—and, I suppose, mine had I looked at it in that light—was that there were two of me, so to speak. Martin John Macdonald and Martin Ian Macdonald. And while the British Army was prepared to let John complete his rather bedraggled career at university it wished Ian to adorn its last batch of National Servicemen. So I sat with an exemption slip in one hand and call-up papers in the other, while across the desk my civil servant was confronted by two sets of documentation stretching back to my early childhood and the seemingly inexorable problem of deciding which of me was which.

Gently, I took him through it again. Iain, I explained, was a Gaelic name. He nodded. John had been its accepted English translation or equivalent for centuries. Again the nod. But down the years Ian, an anglicised form of Iain, had emerged as an English name in its own right. No nod this time, merely a wary inclination of the head. I quickly abandoned a foray down an even more convoluted byway which might or might not ex-plain how every John in the Bible surfaced in Gaelic as Eoin, and went for the clincher. Ergo, Iain = John. Q.E.D.

But not Q.E.D. All the ingrained prejudice of the Edinburgh bureaucracy rankled and rejected the logic. In any case he had his own, more triumphant clincher. Supposing my argument did contain some element of truth, how on earth to explain these? And he waved his hand at the two piles of documents fighting for survival on his desk. I settled in for a long afternoon and moved the scenario to a winter day in Uig, Skye, in late 1937.

Soon after my birth, I explained, Neil Macdonald, crofter and seaman, my father, would have visited my mother in hospital. There was the matter of choosing a name which, given the community's steadfast adherence to family names, was no more than a question of which of my grandfathers' names should take precedence. I emerged from that discussion as Martainn Iain; the Gaelic form simply because Gaelic was my parents' native language. My father would then have visited the local registrar and, quite instinctively following the code that had been thrust upon and accepted by the Gaelic community for generations, would have registered the birth in English. So officially I became Martin John. My mother meanwhile lay in hospital dreaming dreams for her son and if his name figured in those hopeful projections for his future she must have seen it as Martin Ian. Certainly those were the names she gave the schoolmaster and the doctor and anyone else who had call to use them in an official capacity. And when, in my late teens, I discovered the discrepancy between my birth certificate and all my other documents she dismissed it by saying that my father had made a mistake, Ian was the name she had always intended and, in any case, what on earth did it matter?

And in any real sense it did not matter. Except that my civil servant obviously regarded the whole incident as a quite deliberate challenge to all the values of his calling. But it was late Friday afternoon in early summer and the week-end beckoned. So after much grumbling and ostentatious consultation with his colleagues he handed me another document which presumably reconciled my identities. I scribbled my signature and walked into the Edinburgh streets, away from Ian and the British Army. It was a ludicrous incident, and I wondered idly what my civil servant would have made of that much vaster discrepancy between Martainn and Martin, had I tried to explain it. For many of my childhood friends were Martainns within the confines of their native Gaelic community and Martins in school and in the wider world outside, and always the Martainns had to make the essential compromises to bridge the two. Through long conditioning and acceptance the community was no longer conscious of a clash nor, during our

40

schooldays, were we. But looking back I can see that tensions existed between our dual worlds. And since those tensions concerned identity, and identity is crucial, they must have left a mark.

The world of which I gradually became aware during those early years of the war was a crofting township called Achachorc, some two miles from Portree. The crofts were large, the product of a land resettlement scheme in the 'twenties, and the houses straggled in a mile-long ribbon across the hillside. We, my mother and I, lived in the middle of the township in a house belonging to her brother, a bachelor and a captain in the merchant service. My father was also at sea. From time to time they appeared on leave, bringing with them utility toys, brittle aeroplanes and crudely hewn wooden battleships with pins for guns; occasionally they brought more substantial things, rubber wellingtons and a real leather schoolbag smuggled through from the Iceland run. The neighbouring crofters, older men exempt from war, were more frequent visitors. Daily they would bring milk and fresh butter, occasionally they would drop by with a rabbit or hare. On a late autumn morning Niall Choinnich and Seonaidh Beag Anderson would appear to flush a sack of glistening herring on to the kitchen floor after a night's fishing. No crofting township suffered much privation during the war.

There were few visitors from outwith the community. Once a fortnight 'Lady Iona', more properly the Hon. Mrs Macdonald of Portree House, would come to collect for some deserving war charity. She never followed the road. We would see her appear two miles away, over the brow of the hillock that half-hid the roofs of Portree, and we would follow her erratic course up the glen through the bogs and heather till she stood at our door, all tweed suit and knitted stockings and brogues, with a small terrier at her heels. She would sit straight-backed in a chair and my mother would serve her tea in her best china. As regularly Seonaid, the tinker, would appear. She would come along the township road, stopping at every house and maybe spending half an hour in each. She was a small, wiry crow of a woman, bent under a canvas pack, and even then, when she was little more than forty, her face was lined and gnarled and weather-beaten. She and my mother would sit on either side of the fire over a cup of tea and exchange Gaelic chit-chat about births and deaths and marriages. Seonaid carried all the personal gossip that kept the crofting communities in touch with each other.

41

I played with the children next door and with my Glasgow cousins who lived with my grandparents in the last house in the township. The four of them burst upon us as evacuees; aggressive, clamorous kids from the streets of Partick, who understood Gaelic but spoke only Glaswegian. They frightened cattle and swung on gates and left my grandfather waving his stick in impotent rage. They were my first contact with Glasgow but I must have heard of the place before that. The Gaelic ghettoes of Partick and Govan impinge themselves on island consciousness at an early age.

The war was somewhere far-off. An occasional plane would weave a white trail across the summer sky; an American transport plane thundered into the face of Beinn Eadarra and passed into local mythology; Niall Choinnich called one of his dogs Rommel. But only once did the war intrude. One night my mother woke me, wrapped me in blankets, and said she must see Mrs MacLeod about something she had heard on the wireless about a plane crash over Italy. I stood sleepily in the MacLeods' kitchen as the two women keened on each other's shoulders. I was vaguely aware it had something to do with Neil MacLeod who, in the same kitchen a fortnight ago, had allowed me to wear his R.A.F. cap.

I went to school soon afterwards, when in the spring of 1944 we moved to Portree. The distance was only a little over two miles but the communities were very different. Portree was the capital of Skye. In size it may have been a large village with a population of around a thousand, but in plan it was a town. It had a square with solid Victorian buildings; banks, a police station, a court-house, churches, hotels, pubs. It was in fact the quite deliberate creation of a Lord Macdonald of Sleat of the early nineteenth century, who had decreed that the best anchorage in Skye should be the site of the capital. So he had imported builders, masons, carpenters and shopkeepers, and their descendants still formed the core of village society. The crofter people flooded in from the rural areas to provide labour, and the lawyers, bankers, schoolmasters, estate factors and civil servants came from the south to impose an English-speaking bureaucracy. Most of the villagers could speak Gaelic and probably more than half of them did in a domestic situation, but nonetheless it was an English-speaking village. From my limited, childhood perspective it was a warm, tight society. St Valéry had pulled it together; half the young men were in the same German prisoner-of-war camp.

I suppose that we, the generation which attended the village

42

primary school from 1944 till 1950, were a fair reflection of that society. Certainly English was our classroom and playground language and we saw nothing strange in that, though I should imagine that some of us spoke Gaelic at home, and others were spoken to in Gaelic and replied in English. I seem to remember that only those of us from a Gaelic background hung around Danny Fletcher's smithy door, taking turns at blowing the aged leather bellows and listening to the crofters' tales as they waited for the horses to be shod. But I could be wrong. It is some time ago and these were not my pre-occupations then. In any case, if our primary schooling made little acknowledgement of our background, that was not essentially the fault of the non-Gaels amongst us. We received what I presume was a normal Scottish schooling at the time and our community accepted and, indeed, expected that. Our teachers were schooled to give us only that. They were all local women but I never heard any of them, in any circumstance, speak Gaelic. But I suspect some of them must have been able to, long ago, before their schooling started.

Our education was humane, uneventful and unexciting. We scratched on slates, graduated to copy-books, and were occasionally allowed the frivolity of plasticine. Each morning we recited psalms or learned the Shorter Catechism by rote, chanted arithmetical tables, and erupted into the playground, scrabbling for our shinty sticks piled in the corner of the room as we went. That pile of shinty sticks is the one tangible concession to our identity I remember. Historically we learned that Robert the Bruce had an incident with a spider and that King Harold got an arrow in his eye; and geographically, as we moved to the top end of the primary school, we were made aware of those patches on the world map painted red. In our final primary year, the Qualifying Class, we had an Empire Day lecture, and we stood—whether to sing or to ponder in silence, I no longer remember—in honour of that occasion.

At lunchtime we wandered the village streets bickering childishly about our various loyalties to the Church of Scotland, the Free Church or the Free Presbyterian Church. All of them were presbyterian, all of them were Calvinistic, but of course we were not to know that. I imagine we supported them as other kids in other places supported and argued about football teams. In Skye we had heard only of Rangers, but however improbably in those late 'forties, pre-TV days we did know about Rangers.

We stood around the playground squabbling about who was to be Waddell, Thornton, Gillick or Cox. I was always Rutherford or Duncanson. I was rather fat.

Outside the school we jeered at the tinkers as they drunkenly mounted their horses and gigs at their parking lot by the old graveyard. We chanted from house to house at Halloween, and attended our various Sunday schools. We became involved in childish scrapes. We smashed windows and smoked cinnamon sticks and for glorious weeks before we were found out David Forsyth and I stole packets of Gold Flake from his father's corner shop. Ian MacFarlane allowed me to stand self-importantly beside him on the back of his father's delivery lorry which attended the arrival of the island steamer each night. We manhandled the sacks to the edge of the platform for his father, Davy, to lift into the shops. I think I looked on Davy as a substitute father at that time. He took me to my first picture show, grainy, flickering war-time images on a temporary screen in the Drill Hall.

As the war ended the village became alive and exciting. On VE Day my mother dragged her seven-year-old son to the top of the hill above the bay, and we joined the midnight throng who cheered as a scarecrow Hitler danced on a bonfire, and a vast V of lights stretched across the bay below and two captured German submarines, en route to the naval base at Kyle, lay anchored sullenly by the Black Rock at the harbour mouth. The prisoners came home. I stood among the uncomprehending group of children in the square as thin, uncertain men stepped from the buses to be engulfed by our weeping, laughing elders. We swaggered behind pipe bands that sprang from nowhere and stood on the slipway to greet the liberty boats from the grey naval ships that appeared in the bay. We learned to chant, 'any gum, chum?'

I cannot remember the day my father came home, but I can remember the day we expected him to arrive. A man who must have looked the way I wanted my father to look passed the kitchen window, and I surged out of the door and clung to his knees. It took several minutes for my mother to make me under-stand he was only a passing salesman. But my father did come home and that summer of 1946 was as perfect a time as I can remember. He found work at the local salmon fishery, newly re-opened after the war, and the other fishermen's sons and I spent the summer around the harbour. We fished and sailed and ferried men from boat to shore; each afternoon we joined the boat crew on the coastal trip to gather the salmon from the bag-nets, hindering as much as we helped, I suppose, but feeling adult and important. And we silently clung to every word as the men talked on the way back to harbour, listened to them as we had never listened to a teacher.

It was not meant to last, of course. A seasonal job and a rented house was no security, and I gradually became aware of a continuous debate between my father and mother about the future. To stay in Portree? Or a break for Glasgow? Or a croft, perhaps . . .? There was a holiday in Glasgow, my first trip to the mainland. The coastal steamer was no novelty, but I should have been agawk with excitement at trains and trams and double-deck buses. Yet I can recall none of them. I am left with an impression of vast, scarred, masonry-tumbled gaps in the tenements, the Saturday night smell of fish and chip shops, the moment of panic when my parents hid in a close to see my reaction, and the confident, strident packs of children in the streets. They swarmed over the air-raid shelters outside my aunt's house in Partick, and I pressed my nose to the window-pane and longed to have the confidence to join them.

Eventually it was a croft, the one next to my uncle's in Achachorc, Seonaidh Beag Anderson's croft. He had left to set up shop in Portree. Achachorc was essentially the same as when we had left it five years earlier; some of the older people had died, a couple of families had moved out, but my grandparents still stayed in the end house and Niall Choinnich still had the dog called Rommel. The school car now picked me up each morning and dropped me on my doorstep each evening, so my involvement with my peers was reduced to the fleeting contact of school hours. The street corner gangs of an evening gave way to the chores that a croft demands even of children; cleaning oil lamps, stacking peats, bringing the cows home for milking, feeding calves and hens. Work and leisure merged imperceptibly with each other. We did indeed meet to kick a ball around, or play shinty or even—improbably in that environment—cricket; and on Saturday we might cycle down to Portree to watch a shinty match and, in the evening, to attend the pictures in the Drill Hall. But on the whole, perhaps because there were so few of us—only four or five, and of disparate ages—our games tended towards spontaneous sessions of Cowboys and Indians as we drove the cattle home. And if the men set up a counter-attraction like a sheep-shearing or a muir-burning we homed in on it to play as much part as they would allow us. Essentially our pleasures fringed on the adult activity of the township.

In that environment everyone spoke Gaelic; it was the language of the home and of the sheep-fank. Mine had probably grown rusty during the years in Portree but at least I had retained it, probably through frequent visits to my grandparents—my grandmother spoke only a smattering of stilted English—and through that summer with the fishermen. But it was not proof against the more robust usage of the township. Niall Choinnich laughed me to scorn when I sent a shepherd in the wrong direction to look for a strayed ram simply because my vocabulary was inadequate. I was made aware that two languages existed, and I determined never to be laughed to scorn again.

I became aware also of the township hill, the sprawling moorland acres that rose from behind the crofts to the heather peaks of the Corr-bheinn and Beinn a' Chearcaill, and broke off in scree slopes to the river valley and rose again to the sheer sea-cliffs facing the Wester Ross mainland. It was a vast, unpeopled hill, and yet the remains of villages were dotted all over it, with the dry-stone walls of the houses still at shoulder height, as the people had left them when they were driven out in the 1850s. I walked the hill frequently with my father at lambing time. We would eat our lunch in the lee of a rock, inadequately sheltered against the driving rain, and I learned where the fresh-water springs were, and where the stone was where the shepherds had carved their names down the years, and how my grandfather had first come there as a shepherd for the estate before 1900. In late impressionable adolescence I walked that same hill with the shotgun, ostensibly hunting for rabbits or foxes, but in reality willing a man from 1850 to walk over the brow of the next hillock and sit with me and talk. I knew we would know each other. It never happened, of course.

In 1950 my primary education ended. Almost without noticing it, and certainly without any consultation between the school and my parents, I slipped into an academic course in Portree Secondary School. The primary and secondary school were under the same roof and shared the same headmaster, but the secondary school had an intake of academic pupils from the whole of Skye and from the Inverness-shire isles of the Outer Islands. Half my primary school friends disappeared into what was known as

46

the practical stream, essentially a continuation until they were fifteen of their primary curriculum with an *ad hoc* addition of elementary science, domestic science, gardening and woodwork. Inevitably the two groups diverged, socially as well as academically. But even within the academic stream there were niceties of distinction, niceties of which we were not aware at the time but which are certainly clear in retrospect. The choice in modern languages lay between French, Gaelic and Greek; choice euphemistically since few of us were consulted. All the ex-Portree primary pupils automatically arrived in the French class, possibly on the assumption that they did not speak Gaelic but also, I suspect, because of a certain elitism, conscious or otherwise, which demanded that local pupils should be aimed in the most prestigious direction. Certainly the few who joined us there from the rural primary schools were invariably teachers' or ministers' children.

The bulk of the rural pupils from Skye and all the pupils from the Outer Isles were consigned to the Gaelic class, to face the unedifying prospect at twelve years of age of learning to read and write their native language from 'the cat sat on the mat' stage. Each year a sacrificial two or three took Greek. I always understood this to be the mark of an early vocation for the ministry and tended to treat them with the reserve that such an awesome prospect demanded, but recently one of them confided that the real reason was that the system demanded that the classics master should have some class other than Latin to fill his time with.

The rural and island pupils lived a segregated life in the school hostels. They skirmished briefly down the village streets after school and at five o'clock were regimented back to the hostels for tea and study and prayers and bed. On Saturdays they were encouraged to join the school cadets, on Saturday evenings they were allowed to go to the pictures (or confined-to-barracks as punishment) and on Sundays they emerged twice daily as a long disjointed crocodile to split three ways at the village square to their respective churches. In the classrooms they stared silent insolence at those teachers who doubled as hostel wardens with a venom that the rest of us could not understand.

I think I was vaguely aware that my life had passed some kind of critical turning point. Certainly the township acknowledged the fact in tiny, subtle ways. Though I still dashed as eagerly as anyone to the fank after school I tended to find myself, quite inexplicably, on the periphery of its activities while my friends, most of them younger and all of them in the practical stream at school, milled around where the action was. They were actively taught to shear, to gather, to castrate the lambs, while I stood around catching the occasional stray sheep or packing fleeces; useful, yes, but traditionally the work of old men and young boys. I was no longer in the mainstream of township life and, long before I realised it, the township, by instinctive, conditioned consent, had assumed that our paths would diverge; and made my way easy.

At home neighbours and visitors would say to my mother in that knowing, adult way that allows grown-ups to discuss children as if they were not present, 'Se sgoilear math a th'ann, tha e coltach?' And my mother would admit with a nice degree of modesty that, yes, I was not too bad a scholar if I would only work and that I hoped to go in for the ministry. Against all the evidence my mother refused to believe otherwise for many years. Though she herself subscribed to a benevolent evangelism which allowed her to be a communicant of the Church of Scotland, attend few services, and believe that all human beings, including atheists, were striving towards God in their various ways, I suspect her wish was as much an expression of social aspiration as it was of piety. Certainly when, in the throes of teenage rebellion, I stood facing my father and my mother and the Free Kirk elder, blankly refusing to sign a Sabbatarian petition, I realised that while I might be guilty of a considerable breach of etiquette, in the eyes of my parents I was not guilty of blasphemy. And when, in the mid-'fifties, I succumbed to Radio Luxembourg's 'Top Twenty' at 11 p.m. on a Sunday night their remonstrances seemed to stem more from convention than conviction . . .

In any case, through my childish eyes, religion in our township reduced itself to a few easily assimilated Sabbath taboos. You avoided Free Presbyterian households on Sunday; you passed the time of day, soberly, with Free Kirkers on their way to church in Portree; and you took to the hills, unobtrusively, with the Church of Scotland kids and your Free Kirk cousins. Kinship smashed taboos. Organised games were out, but on a hill as wide as that no one needed them.

Sunday was also—always had been—the day for visiting my grandparents. I would come down from the hill at dusk to their house at the end of the township and immerse myself between the blue wrappers of the weekly edition of the *Bulletin* that had arrived from my aunt in Partick. I devoured the minutiae of the Christie murder trial, as much of it as could decently be printed in those days, and wondered at the implications of what had been left out. Later in the evening my father would arrive, and my grandmother would begin to talk. She was a small, strong woman, hunched with arthritis, and at an age to reminisce. Her memory for incident and anecdote was clear and concise and she could recount, word for word, conversations which had taken place in the 'eighties of the previous century. Her mind was untrammelled by formal schooling and she had a gift for the verbal evocation of character and incident. She never attempted to interpret them or evaluate them in any wider context than that of the village community of her youth.

What emerged from those Sunday evening sessions, that continued as circumstances allowed till I was in my mid-twenties, was a social and, I eventually realised, a political history of the people to whom I belonged. The realisation came gradually, of course. In my early teens my grandmother's tales were no more to me than adventure stories, vividly told, with the added bonus that most of the characters were related to me, or if not to me, to someone I knew. Her cotter community, thrown on to half-acre plots on the shores of Kilmuir by the Clearances, was a fertile source of anecdote. Her father's seven years on Clydeside with never a letter home since he could not write, but always the boll of oatmeal on the monthly steamer to feed his family as an earnest of his, and their, survival; her uncle's escape from the breadline of nineteenth-century Skye to the comparative security of the Hong Kong police; her own youthful harvest trips to the stubble fields of Lothian and Easter Ross to earn pittances with a sickle. The picture emerged of a community which had managed to retain a kernel of human dignity against the grinding repression of poverty and active persecution.

One night I stumbled on the fact that a great-grand-uncle had spent weeks in Edinburgh's Calton Jail. Why? Because of the Land League, my grandmother said. The Land League? Yes, when the crofters eventually rose against the landlords and burnt the haystacks, and the detested Sheriff Ivory stalked through the island at the head of the police and the Royal Marines. She told it as she had seen it as a girl of twelve. The police advancing on the houses with the eviction notices, the solid line of Marines

49

behind with rifles at the ready, and, facing them, the defiant women of the township, armed with hayforks, and cod-lines with vicious hooks, and dung, and anything that came to hand.

I had stumbled on the submerged, I now think suppressed, history of the people. At school, of course, no mention was made of it; our formal history, in as much as it had local connotations, stopped with a brief, conventional reference to Culloden. There had, after all, been a battle and thus it deserved an aside in the progress from the rantings and squabblings of medieval kings to the grander canvas of imperial conquest. My grandmother never spoke of Culloden or Prince Charlie; I suspect that to her he was as remote and mythical a figure as Cuchullin. But she had seen the Marines stand against her people, and she remembered that.

It took some years for me to assimilate the pictures she conjured from a not too distant past. There were ambivalent loyalties within the community. The Glendale Martyr, and 'Parnell' Stewart and the other Land League leaders were folk heroes, but mention of the Cameron Highlanders could still rouse a village audience to fervour, and frequently did at the general elections. At fourteen I pored over an official pictorial history of the war and thrilled that men like MacKenzie King and Menzies and Smuts should summon an entire empire to arms the moment Britain was threatened. I still counted red spots on the map. But then, had I not been taught to?

My rebellion, when it came, was largely a teenage exercise in self-assertion. Apart from the set-to with the petitioning elder I decided at fifteen that I would not return to school. Not because I particularly hated school but because I wanted to go to sea. But my mother said no, her father had been at sea, her husband had been at sea, her brother was at sea, and her only son was not going to sea. I argued vehemently and eventually achieved a compromise. It was arranged that I should spend the six weeks of the summer holidays as galley-boy on my uncle's ship, the Outer Isles mail steamer *Loch Seaforth*, and then we would see.

So I joined my uncle, a man whom I loved; who had sailed the world's trade routes since the First War, who had returned thankfully to the security of MacBrayne's during the depression years, and had then taken his ship to Dunkirk and along the Iceland convoy routes in the last war. He stayed with us when on leave and constantly supplied me with books and brochures and pamphlets of sea lore that were much more entrancing than anything school had to offer. As a child I had spent week-ends with him on the *Loch Seaforth*. Now I spewed over greasy dishes in the hot, swaying galley and was invited on to the bridge on Sunday to clean his boots and go out to dine with his friends. Seasickness can be easily overcome but it needs a particularly thick skin to withstand the constant innuendo of city-hardened galley-boys when your uncle is Captain and the Chief Steward lets it be known that you are a cousin. After a fortnight I retired defeated. What had been offered as a compromise had turned out to be an exercise in family complicity.

Since there seemed to be nothing else to do I returned to school somewhat shamefacedly. If it was not over-exciting at least it was tolerable and I seemed to fulfil the main function of passing exams adequately if with little distinction. Few of us seemed to have any idea where we were going but at least that allowed the school to concentrate on feeding as many of us into university as it possibly could. Once there, presumably, we would find a direction. In any case that did not seem to be the school's business. Our Latin master did stop us in our tracks one day by suggesting that we should not enter teaching unless we felt a positive commitment to it but that is the only time I can recall hearing it implied that our education might have some purpose. The rest was based on assumption. I suspect he saved a few of us from disaster.

We assimilated facts, or not, as they were presented to us, and tried to divert the more amenable teachers into interesting conversational backwaters to relieve the boredom. We relished the Friday afternoons when we could persuade the English master to give a reading of Thurber for his and our enjoyment. But those moments were few. For the rest we regurgitated what was offered to us. During break we scuffled idly through the school corridors arguing the merits of the latest Dean Martin or Frankie Lane release, till the day Bill Haley burst upon us. Then we went home to argue hopelessly with our parents that drainpipe trousers and thick crepe soles were necessary props to our self-respect. During the mid-fifty years Portree, the town, began to exert a strong counter-pull to Achachorc, the crofting township, largely, I suspect, because it offered girls who were not the familiar girls next door. Certainly the attraction of fank and hill remained strong, but the Saturday night picture show in the village took on a new urgency and could lead to some promising contacts with the hostel girls on the way home.

So we emerged into our sixth and final year, a broad stream vaguely en route to university since that seemed to be what was expected of us. Most of us had only one or two Higher certificates to pass for our entrance qualifications but since Portree School had neither library accommodation nor post-Higher teaching facilities we were euphemistically allocated 'free periods' which we were expected to pass studying quietly in the back row of any class whose teacher would tolerate us. Since Third Year had a fair percentage of presentable girls who were just becoming aware of older males we normally followed them.

We quickly adapted to the system and exploited it. We learned when it was possible to scuttle out of school unseen and take the back lane to the village. It was an enjoyable year. Our new freedom allowed us to make contact with each other at a level that had not been possible in the regimented classrooms and in the partitioned domestic circumstances of hostel, village and crofting township. On one of these village trips Donald Macdonald, Uist-born and hostel-bred, responded in some surprise to some chance remark of mine that he had not known I spoke Gaelic. As fluently as he did, I said. Donald Michie, country-born and village-bred, said that his mother said that he had spoken only Gaelic at first but he had lost it now and could not even understand it. It was a small moment of minor discovery and we hurried to the café to drink coffee and eye the waitresses.

The headmaster sent for me. With him was Kenny Angus, son of Niall Choinnich from Achachoc, three years my junior. 'You both speak Gaelic?' the headmaster said. We nodded. In that case would we please try to find the Nicolson twins from Glenmore who had just run away for the fourth time in their first few weeks in primary school. And would we do it as discreetly as possible. They spoke no English, he explained, and the other children in their class had laughed at them. He did not add that their teacher spoke no Gaelic.

So on that day in our school life, for the purposes of the school, Kenny Angus and I reverted briefly to being Coinneach Neill Choinnich and Martainnn Neill Iain Mhoir. We stumbled over the rough moorland towards the massive bulk of Suidhe Fhinn that separated the glen from the school. We found them some miles away where the hill became steep. Two tearful, lonely

52

children, clutching each other by the hand, facing the immense mountain that lay between them and security. And we, of their people, cajoled and gentled them back into the system that had so oppressed them.

In that same year, 1956, I left school. Prize-givings, I should imagine, are much the same throughout Britain; the earnest, unctuous speeches, the solemn, over-dressed parents, the unimpressed pupils. A minister made the speech in the professionally mournful voice of Hebridean pulpits. We were now leaving our school and our island to make our way in the wider world; most of us would return only for brief visits; but our school and our island would never forget us; and we must never bring shame on our school and our island. I knew the speech was aimed solely at us, the departing academic elite of sixth year, for many of those of the practical stream who were leaving at fifteen would remain on the island to sustain the community. But our school had little to do with the sustenance of the community; it was essentially an alien plan to tap us for another community. And there lay the difference between our prize-giving and most other prize-givings in Britain that day. Those others might aspire to be a celebration of a transitional stage within a community; for most of us ours was a ritual for transferring a body of people from one community to another. Our Gaelic community could take us no further than the fank or the fishing boat or the hill, it was implied. Nor was it encouraged to.

At Edinburgh University I quickly sought the cover of the Highland student community. We sat around the common room talking Gaelic occasionally, talking English frequently from our own uncertainty, for the comfort of those of us in whom education had corroded fluency, and for the acceptance of the stray Lowlanders, Yorkshiremen, Welsh and Cockneys who inexplicably gravitated towards us.

October 1956 was a good time to be in Edinburgh. Suez was on the boil and Hungary was an unseen shaft on the horizon. As the debate grew heated in the common room I found that an education at Portree Secondary School seemed to provide inadequate armament for argument, even on the fringes. My tentative mouthings about red spots on the map were never heard, and those who could make such views heard spoke from a background and with accents that were alien to me. I stood bewildered in the Old Quad and watched uncomprehendingly as the

53

mob writhed, and Victor Davis, pacifist, smashed a fist in pacific wrath in an opponent's face, and two American gentlemen, post-graduate students, stood deadpan in pork-pie hats, not two feet away from the furore, with a placard which proclaimed simply 'I like Ike'.

As that week progressed the violence in Old Quad swelled and overflowed into the street, to be contained by the police, and for an illusory moment students in Edinburgh almost believed they might be as effective in British politics as their continental counterparts were in Europe. That feeling died, of course, but as I came out of it the red spots faded and I found myself groping darkly towards a definition of some instinctively felt connection that linked those major atrocities in Hungary and Whitehall with that other atrocity that had placed a great-grand-uncle of mine in a jail on the Edinburgh skyline. During two years of talk and drink and enjoyment in Edinburgh (and of negligible academic progress) I discovered that a poet called Sorley MacLean, who wrote in a language I knew well, had travelled far on that same road.

The summers, the Easters, the New Years and the Christmases, I spent in Skye; working for the Post Office, working for farmers, working on the croft. When I was twenty-one years of age Niall Choinnich taught me to shear; a belated recognition of maturity in my own community. I made contact with the boys who had left school at fifteen and we wandered the village dance-halls. In Skeabost, Uig, Dunvegan, Broadford and Portree we shared half-bottles of whisky in cars, and discovered other grandmothers who had talked to grandsons. We wondered why our parents had not spoken to us of the same things. We had heard of two world wars and of economic circumstances but we knew nothing of the reality.

In 1960 I returned to Edinburgh, to a good year. A class in Celtic gave some formal recognition to my background, and a class in Imperial and American History opened my mind to the world. The lecturer in that class, George Shepperson, insisted on having one of each nationality in his tutorials to provide fertile discussion. And he insisted, where possible, on having two Scots; one Lowlander and one Gael. There is something more than ironic in being processed through an educational system to the age of twenty-one before your identity is recognised. But even at that age such recognition instils some measure of confidence. Enough at least to tell an Edinburgh civil servant that John = Ian. Q.E.D.

BOB TAIT

Take Me to the Station

Take me to the Station
And put me on the train.
I got no expectation
To pass through here again.
Rolling Stones

An important part of anyone's life is the point where they reckon they passed out of a relatively protective range of childhood influences. That point for me lay on a railway line. Of course, I didn't know that at the time, and must have run clickety-click back and forward over it for most of a year.

It was the year I travelled up and down nearly every day between Kilmarnock, Ayrshire, and Glasgow: first year at Glasgow University, I was eighteen, and had just left St Joseph's Roman Catholic High School in Kilmarnock. It was the winter of 1961-62.

Ancient steam locomotives still pulled that 7.03 a.m. local train haltingly through the small towns of north Ayrshire and Renfrewshire to St Enoch's station, and took an hour or so about it. In the wintry mist of the half-lit station, the dark shadowy bulk of the engine leaked and hissed, half-shrouding itself and the carriages behind it. It was a daily re-evocation of the other most important terminal in my childhood: Galashiels, tucked away in the faraway Border hills, much further away from the world I've been living in since 1961 than mileages can express. But in the old days, the massive locos that fussed and thundered from Edinburgh to Gala and the south, on the last leg of our long jaunts via Glasgow and Edinburgh back 'home' (as my mother would say), were a vital part of a whole other-world of my childhood: a complete alternative kind of existence to our life in Kilmarnock.

For this other journey, our bunch of student commuters would pack themselves tightly into one or two of the separate wooden compartments (there were no corridors on those carriages), pull the worn leather straps that held the window shut and kept you reasonably free from draughts if you were lucky, and hope we wouldn't also have to chip ice off the inside of the glass that morning.

We packed in for warmth, and quickly got to know each other. We hadn't all gone to the same school. Looking around the compartment, I see what had happened. A majority of us had been at Kilmarnock Academy all those years: the rest of us were Catholics. It had hardly struck us: that the difference meant there were so many of about the same age and similar kinds of interests in a small town whom you didn't get to know at all until eventually you met on the road out of it.

Outside the station, but pointing the opposite way to the one I was going, lay a high stone viaduct. As we pulled away, one or two would maybe already be singing 'The Wreck of the Old 97', or some other such train song or travelling song, in fair imitation of Lonnie Donegan. Donegan was the inspiration for many a skiffle group throughout Scotland's very own West, but nowhere more so than among the rangy mining-town cowboys up the Ayrshire valleys on the other side of that viaduct. It was with people there and with people from there that I remember having some of the most memorable times as a kid growing through adolescence: with their open and easy-going faces and manners, with their big families, their families from 'way back, their open doors, their confident acceptance of strangers in their midst. Not too many of them would be heading north with me, away from that world, even as far as Glasgow—not then, anyway.

It was possible, too, to look over the sheer drop of the viaduct at the gaunt and graceless hulk of a Model Lodging House for Men in the derelict Foregate, a building which had briefly housed part of our school, and which for me, at the earlier point of transition from early childhood to adolescence, had proved to be another kind of junction-cum-signal box where people dispersed and began to go their separate ways.

That was the old town-centre of Kilmarnock, symbolised as much as anything by the central importance of a roundabout which distributed people and traffic throughout industrial and rural Ayrshire, separated from the density of Glasgow's common woes and struggles by the bleak and empty Fenwick Moor to the

56

north. That old centre is gone: the distribution system has widened to a system of by-passes. And now they have a new centre, a conglomerate of shops, multi-storey parking and a bus station, with one big warehouse of a pub down in its depths instead of the sprinkling of relatively cosy wee ones. Even as I write this, I hear on the radio that the new centre has just had its formal opening celebrations—and that only about 4,000 people bothered to turn up. You could find about 4,000 folk doing this, that and the other in the middle of Kilmarnock any wet Monday morning. I emphasise 'only' because this is the centre of a greatly grown 'conurbation' now, and because it reflects a longstanding aspect of twentieth-century Kilmarnock. It has not been a place to inspire hearty impulses to share in communal celebrations, concerns and intimacies. Nor does the new cold centre in any way inspire that for the future.

In fact, this is really a story about arrivals and departures, about people who only half fit in anywhere and who leave only half knowing each other—and about the 1944 Education Act to boot. And it is about how I think I was caught up in all that.

I got caught up in a distribution mechanism in two main ways. First of all, I was brought up in the kind of industrial town where people come in and out on waves of employment and unemployment, like my own parents. Life and work then split them up in apparently arbitrary kinds of ways and never really provide a basis of widely, communally shared and understood problems or interests. The people you meet because they attend the same church or denominational school, or go to the same work—well, you probably know some of them better than you know your neighbours, but not actually in a very neighbourly kind of way either. It's not that people are normally unhelpful or sour. It's more that they are often just not there. Doors are often only half open, and you'd want to be sure you were invited. People politely expect the same defensive, private reflex in you. It even effects families. A son marries and moves. His mother is apt to take it for granted that she has to be asked round. Life and work is structured to encourage various kinds and levels of dispersal. And a fair amount of actual moving is endemic: changing houses and localities, jobs, and indeed towns. I'm not suggesting that the population is abnormally unstable, just that it was and is, when all is said and done, incohesive. And no one has to move far, in any case, for this semi-isolating effect to set in. My parents, who have recently retired, still live there after forty years of it. Recently they've been meeting up with people they used to live beside maybe twenty or thirty years ago. They now share nostalgia about some things. But what else? For where were those same people during so much of their working lives? Perhaps not more than a couple of miles away, and yet . . . So partly what I'm writing about is: losing touch as a way of life. Which people considered quite 'normal', of course: that is, they usually wouldn't stop to consider it at all.

The other main sense in which I think I was caught up in a kind of distribution mechanism was through the distributor effect of the education system: a socialising process that selected routes for all without consideration of the need for good roots. The religious segregation of State schools in Scotland is, of course, one of the most remarkable, if not notorious, aspects of our social scene. So, for a start, you found yourself in separate hothouses. Then, in general, it was a system concerned with sorting out as finely as possible how you would earn a living, but not with where you earned it or with whom. It was for moving you all on your separate courses out into the world, not for helping you to converge in a social or working sense: not really concerned with how people might forge communities together, or fail to.

So there we all are, jumbled together on this train: those few of us who have joined that part of our generation custom-built for mobility: for a world of shifting occupations, for mobile nuclear families—and their explosions. We didn't know about that. Our new-found student camaraderie was real. True, when we got to Glasgow, we'd usually go our very different ways and only meet back on the train at night. There were so many new people, new possibilities in life. Looking around the compartment again at a particular group who regularly contrived to cram in together, I see the three blokes I'd come to feel closest to in our final year or two at school. Last heard of, one of them was in the Middle East. The second, with whom I'd a lot in common, including a passion for blue-grass, skiffle and blues, was killed a couple of years later, a death which did a lot to sever any feeling I had of connection with people of my age in my own home town. The third still lives near it, I believe, but, note, not in it. We had no idea what kind of distances there were in the world we were moving into so quickly. The word deracination wasn't one of our words.

To be honest, what I thought I knew about remaining 'part

58

of the community' I didn't care for one bit. As far as I could see, it meant living a life entirely innocent of any intellectual curiosity or excitement. A deadening matter-of-fact-ness seemed to blanket what nearly everyone said or did: when and how and where they got jobs; what kind of jobs they went after and got; when and how they got married; what they did about a house; how they furnished it; what happened next, and so on, like that; and then the final, dull, uncommunicative sound of the door closing when a coffin left. I reckon I was just reacting (in no very original way, of course) to one of the fifty-seven varieties of drab, de-sexualising, defensive and yet complacent-looking cans of respectable good living which you can lift off the shelves of middle-class city suburbs and work-class conurbations alike.

I was also, in a sense, well rehearsed for moving on in relatively deep isolation. Accidents of birth, illness and family circumstances had seen to that. The rehearsal started with my very earliest experiences. After a breech birth which nearly did for both participants, it was found I was jaundiced (already). What to do? As in all good comic strips, an unlikely solution popped up. An incubator was a fairly new-fangled gadget at the time, one which you might not expect to find in an obscure wee maternity hospital in the middle of the war, at some distance from the scientific and military front lines.

So there I was for my first months, in a kind of space capsule, a satellite existence, remote from direct human contact, in a strange artificial light, life functions carefully controlled and directed, both extraordinarily vulnerable and extraordinarily protected and insulated. Then, between the time they signed my release from there and signed me up into the school system, I'd had pneumonia a couple of times, had my tonsils out, and also been back in hospital for a mastoid that burst deep in one ear and nearly fatally damaged adjacent parts.

The pneumonia was dealt with mainly by a drug we always simply referred to as M and B. It has hallucinatory side effects. At least, I can assure you that it had hallucinatory effects on me. Actual infant experiences blend in with memories of a not always very gently psychedelic nature: the qualities rather than the facts of life at the time. It may not be entirely coincidental that my favourite philosopher is still the eighteenth-century Scotsman, David Hume, to whom the human self seemed basically nothing more than a loose bundle of perceptions. The other side of that

59

bleak overall perception, of course, is the precarious and provisional nature of the order we can achieve for ourselves, individually and collectively, in the world: an order dependent on human creativity and constructiveness.

Meanwhile, my mother and father had a hard job ensuring my survival. They had come to Kilmarnock just before the war so that my father could find work. They felt very cut off from real family life, since there were only three of us, and from the kind of Borders communities they had known. Fortunately, a few similarly placed 'Expatriates' lived nearby in the clutter of tenements: that had helped. But now, with me on the scene, they joined the general process that accelerated after the war: everyone trying to find their own best way out from an unhealthy centre to a dot in a sprawling periphery.

For the first five years, I was brought up in a tenement that belonged to the next door neighbour: a carpet firm called BMK, then engaged in war work. My father was a loom maintenance man there, out of the forces on health grounds. The main factory was for its time a glamorously tall, white and glassy creation that made me think of stately ocean liners. It stands where it did, beside the smelly little river that runs through the town, roughly parallel with the nearby main street. At one end of our street, the main electricity generating plant hummed and crackled and spat out damp, sulphuric fumes. The streets of red sand-stone tenements were darkened by clouds of sour particles in the air from jute and carpeting, coal and coke. I can still hear the wail of the air-raid siren which BMK continued to use as its factory hooter, the clatter of looms, the rumbling of lorries outside the window where I lay. My mother worked ferociously to keep the house and everything in it and everything on us clean and polished and fresh. At the same time, she kept up an indefatigable campaign of personal lobbying to get us a council house. Eventually, we moved south a mile or so to Maxholm Road, part of a pre-war scheme, then at the edge of town. Later we were re-housed once more, in a new house at a new southerly town boundary.

The price paid for each move is measured in distances which, again, don't figure on milometers. At each step, another set of briefly established yet surprisingly fragile contacts became tenuous to vanishing point. By the time of the second move, I was off to secondary school, itself newly removed to the *northern* boundary of the town. Your three or four best mates at school

60

lived at various spots miles away, and you couldn't really share them with local pals.

There were very real gains, of course, even in Maxholm Road. Our upstairs flat looked out on fields and the municipal golf course. I could fall in the wee burn and be drowned, if I liked, rather than be instantly poisoned. And in fact, I quickly grew much healthier and stronger there. I could even get out to play football. Not to play football was obviously a terrible social disability, and I had a lot to catch up on, having missed much essential pre-school cultivation of reflexes. I never did catch up. But the other lads usually sympathetically tolerated my efforts.

Nonetheless, a pattern was already established in my life. I was able to spend so many hours on my own, absorbed with my own devices—drawn, painted, written, invented or sung devices—not fretting if I wasn't let out to play because of thunder and lightning, blizzard or drizzle, that I didn't typically fit into the life other kids led in the neighbourhood anyway. And so I wafted along, contentedly enough most of the time in another kind of insulated world, but this time largely of my own design and construction. I got through school in this way, more or less at my own pace. Again, comic strip logic arranged things for me that my interests yielded more certificates of academic good health for me than for most of my contemporaries, who were in some senses more alive to their environments. Up to the time I was boarding the Glasgow train, it was as if life usually came to me as one big present. No past, no future, just a nice big continuous present. To someone like that, even the gradual discovery of human history and the fact that people are seriously affected by it comes as a terrible shock.

It's inevitably with that later perspective in my head that I have to look back on school and religion and all that. Now, as to religion, we were never, as my mother puts it, 'gospel-greedy'. But for more than half our folk, regular mass-going, the rituals of benediction and processions were all an incense-flavoured part of an emotional order. There were rather nasty, guilt-inducing aspects to that. But what really got me in the end about Scottish Catholicism only got to me later, when I came to appreciate how much sickly pietism cloys with special-interest, even ghetto mentalities, in the West of Scotland to produce a reverse mirror image of the drab codes and taboos of Scottish Protestantism. I was glad to get shot of it.

61

All the same, there were certain realities which St Joe's in Kilmarnock was faced with and which, like a Special Defence Corps, the school tried to do something about.

When we lined up on our very first day, or maybe the second, a little boy grabbed me by the hand. I was startled. He was scared. I was no fatty, and not exactly ostentatiously dressed, just reasonably neat. He was skinny and dirty, cold and trembly. The Catholic school had for a long time been called the ragged school. This was what Mr Breen, our headmaster, proposed to do something about.

There were poor Proddies too, of course, who also didn't go to the Academy, which was just across the road from us—although on a notably higher elevation. Its proximity dramatised the problem as perceived by leaders of the Catholic community. Their lot were felt to be at the bottom of the social pile, and therefore needed to have their aspirations upgraded. For a start, they contrived to get St Joseph's called a High School.

Mr Breen's appearance somehow conveyed the impression that his surroundings had been temporarily disarranged by some kind of blitz, and that all would be restored to normal standards of excellence when the cleaners arrived. It certainly took some such feat of imagination to set about founding a crowning academic edifice on the heap of buildings we had to make do with. Even by the time I was in upper primary, heading for secondary, we were housed in that not very convincingly converted Model Lodging House. 'The Model' stood next to a grimy, scarred pub which stuck up like a solitary bad tooth—around which a lot of sour air still hung. We had our playtimes surrounded by the crumbling walls of demolition jobs which somebody had forgotten to finish. Yet, somehow, it was a good time: despite the terrors of weekly Ink Exercises, the dingy, fume-filled metalwork room in 'The Model's' depths, the hazards of packed joinery benches, the discomfort and noisiness of the ordinary classrooms. Harassed teachers must have hated it, but seldom took it out on us. There we mixed and made do: all kinds of kids, all kinds of abilities, learning to make a go of all kinds of things together. Which might have been the beginning of something.

Of course, our airy new buildings on the edge of town were an improvement. The atrocious old facilities had cramped the style of many a teacher and too many children had reached premature turn-off points from the whole business of learning because it couldn't be made an attractive enough proposition. But as we moved on up the road, a mixture of Catholic aspirations and the stern socio-economic logic of the 1944 Education Act scattered us into separate groups once more, albeit at last under the same roof.

The push for higher academic achievements and the raising of occupational sights didn't really take on. Exhorted to greater efforts by church and school, most went through the motions with a lack of conviction and a faint air of bewilderment, and the Highers exam classes remained sparsely populated in proportion to our numbers. We split into smaller penny numbers than that. Out with school sport activities and dances, and, bizarrely, our versions of Gilbert and Sullivan, those whose interests accidentally coincided went off and coincided. Because of the religious and geographical scatter, there wasn't so much of that, either, after four. You might catch a few of us making a meal of a cup of coffee in the middle of town. We hoped you wouldn't catch us experimentally defying God and the Lady Adviser with the girls in the Kay Park. But what were we collectively up to or aiming for? There wasn't even a coherent counter-culture to suggest what. Instead, at the end of the last school day, came a moment whose meaning many had tacitly understood and anticipated all along: dispersal into a world whose job offers and other courses on offer lay dotted in not very comprehensible pattern before us—but so inevitably, and so unopen to comment or discussion.

Even to a child's mind and eye, when the train pulled into Galashiels station, he'd arrived in a different kind of world. The little town lay in a bowl made for it by the Border hills and Gala water. From any one of the slopes you could see what the mills and streets, shops, schools and parks had to do with each other, and how they converged on the clock tower of the town hall with its dramatic statue of Border reivers. The life of town and country, of time past and time present, converged. They used to say that everyone knew each other, which wasn't true, fortunately. But there were fewer actual barriers and limits to common knowledge and intimacy. Certainly, you found that within a generation of leaving Derry and Drogheda in Ireland, Dunns, Dochertys and Taits—our lot there—were interwoven with Lothian and Border families in a texture as intricate as the local tweed, as strong and real in history and lore as the meeting of the waters of Gala and Tweed.

From the station, we'd go a few hundred yards back along the

c*   63

side of the track to Gran and Grandpa Tait's house: actually a converted pub, with a long, dark, sloping corridor where they used to roll the beer down to the big room at the back. The tradition wasn't entirely lost, rather transformed, especially at Hogmanay, when the old man would lead family, friends and neighbours in from the street, dancing behind his melodeon. He'd been an itinerant farmhand, till they'd got tired of that shifting life, and moved a big family in to an incredibly wee house. He looked as if every feature and limb had been whittled down by the winds. He always sat on a hard wooden chair by the fire, his pipe competing with its smoke output. The thin polished spars and surfaces of the chair faithfully portrayed him when he was out. Gran Tait was as round as he was thin, strong, and built for hugging kids. I knew a lot worried her; I now know some of what did. But she had a talent for enjoying and celebrating anything that gave relief: and having family and friends around her, and their friends too, was a huge satisfaction that called for celebration any day or night of the week. So out came the melodeon. Papa and his melodeon wheezed and grunted out the dance tunes more or less in time with each other, till he'd maybe stop, scowl, throw his bunnet and give somebody a swearing for making an arse of it. That usually had everybody collapsing in a helpless, heaving, hooting mass. Then a more or less solemn offering of whisky to mollify himself. And a new chord set everyone off again. Even when I was too young, tucked up early in bed, and only able to savour the sounds of it all, I came to understand what open house meant. And on the other side of the family, I caught something of the same, time and time again, especially at Uncle Joss McPartlin's house, where we usually stayed, and who had married my mother's eldest sister, Anne Dunn.

Granny Dunn died when I was four, Grandpa long before I was born. I'm told she could recall famine in Drogheda. A photo shows her as an erect old lady, with silky hair, bright eyes, her features fine-lined, serenely smiling, chin up. She had brought up a dozen, mostly on her own, through war and the hungry twenties and thirties. She gave them all as much education as she could afford or pass on herself, being largely self-taught herself, and remarkably widely read. Three of her daughters still live in the town. Even by my time, the family 'tradition' (if you can call it that, when it was more of an imposition) for moving on was re-asserting itself, thinning out the Gala weave: it's loosened out entirely now, and what I experienced was not, after all, to endure.

And it's not something to idealise, for it *couldn't* endure. Such people, strong as they often were, didn't have the resources to hold that kind of collective experience together or make it flourish wider. Nor should the poverty be romanticised, or the cramping of horizons which they suffered from: the narrowing of minds, the boozing, the jealousies and anxieties. As to all of these things, my family, like others, are both victims and agents. I was just lucky enough to glimpse possibilities of co-operation and shared culture which they didn't manage to sustain and spread in a society whose pressures work against the healthy and long-term flourishing of such common knowledge and pooled skill and experiences. But while it lasted . . .

Uncle Joss, badly gassed in World War One, lasted. For forty more years. He was the gentlest and most humorous man I have ever known: mill-worker, artist, good listener, convivial talker, and—though he would have been incredulous to hear this—the man whose examples of openness, patience and generosity with people seem to me still at the heart of something I more fleetingly glimpsed elsewhere, up among mining folk in Ayrshire. There, un-like in Kilmarnock, they managed to create conditions from which they brought understanding and patience and tirelessness together to weld the historic unity that sustained and perhaps ultimately ex-plains Keir Hardie and others who have voiced the values of Scot-tish socialism. Kilmarnock has still to get it together, its labourism never nourished by that kind of human content and contact.

Looking back, I think I see that it is tensions between the polarities in my own make-up, two opposed dimensions of human involvement, that makes me sense so strongly now the need and the possibility of something other than what we have grown used to by way of a 'normal' human relationships and a 'normal' order of interchange and control. And, finally, I can't help seeing that. Myself, in the back yard at Grandpa Tait's, about seven years old. It's pouring rain. Never mind about getting pneumonia again. I'm too fascinated by the giant engines, grinding and belching, surging and slipping on wet metal, as they haul brightly lit trains out of the station. I learn their names off by heart, learn to draw them, guts and all, with reasonable accuracy, glorying in a sense of their power, soon to burst at high speed through mists and valleys, and on and on. But, of course, I didn't really know what trains were all about then.

65

ALLAN MASSIE

Retrospective

To look back . . . there ought to be images, snapshots from a Box Brownie . . . they seem few . . . instead? . . . there are feelings in the air.

Sometimes there is no connection with the child from whom the present I has grown. I can begin to recognise the adolescent, am aware how his choices helped to form me, can review myself in his weaknesses, his speciousness and resent his inability to overcome his defects. Yet even that adolescent, me at sixteen say, is essentially a creation of the me that writes. He never existed as I write him down now till the act of writing. The adolescent who fathered me was not what I might choose to make him. So, in all autobiography there is something of fiction. My past this year is not the same as last. We invent ourselves as we go along; man's life is a novel in progress and it is not only the future that is to be created.

One can look for the truth in Malraux's imaginary museum; even that may turn out to be a hall of moving mirrors.

The past I write down today then is then the past for today.

Geographically my world was still enough. Childhood on Donside; there is an after-harvest gold turning to grey melancholy about the Don and the river is seen in slanting rain as it winds through the haughs. Migrating geese crop the fields by the water. Swans, I early learned, will drown ducks, apparently for fun. Of farming stock, brought up in the hard-won farmland of Aberdeenshire, slowly coming now to an ability to express an admiration for farmers, long-felt though hidden, I was absolutely prevented by a combination of conceit and insufficiency from ever aspiring to farm. My education took place in a society which declared it was more worthy of an ambitious intellect to practise law than agriculture. I was to back away from the Law fast enough, but no nearer the farm. It stands for the good recognised but not pursued.

So, very early on, the retreat into the imagination. My first night at Prep School I read, desperately, as often already, Henty's *In Freedom's Cause: A Tale of Wallace and Bruce*. The ostensible message was simple; the spider's. But I also learned how things could be made true on the page. (Other Hentys were at hand to warn me bookishness could be dangerous.) I blithely ignored the contradiction. Henty after all was capable of preparing his readers to defend the Empire on the North-West Frontier by heroic tales of the Wars of Independence fought against English Imperialism. Clearly that didn't confuse him; why should it worry me? It is not the best books that help form one, but he was soon replaced by better: Dumas, Buchan, Stevenson and Anthony Hope. They all offered journeys, heroes with a certain style – for a long time Rupert of Hentzau was what I'd have liked to be. Buchan and Stevenson gave something more; a clearer scent of the heather than I got surrounded by moors. 'Am I no a bonnie fighter?' asked Alan Breck; admiration for the impossible little man always rises to overcome dislike.

There's a photograph, me aged about eleven. The trousers don't fit the way they're worn, my hair sticks out straight like a flue-brush, my mouth trembles, the eyes look alive. It looks like someone who would come apart easily; you couldn't trust a boy of that sort either. About then, perhaps a year later, I had a Napoleon complex. I appointed other boys, and even the masters who taught me, Marshals of the Empire. I outgrew Napoleon I'm glad to say. He's a lot less convincing than Alan Breck.

Academically precocious; excellently taught at that Prep School, Drumtochty Castle; relying more on flair than solidity though always better at Latin Unseens than Proses. Old-fashioned in the thoroughness of my education, one of probably the last generation to know the Bible as a Text. That gives me a link with the historic Scotland most young Nationalists don't have. It means I feel Scotland is properly a Calvinist country and there is dignity and beauty in the Scots Kirk, however far I've travelled from it. What do we mean by Calvinism when we speak of Scotland? Not merely the beastliness of Predestination and Holy Willie's Prayer. The image is the Kirk in the moorlands, man face to face with God; *reductio ad simplicitatem*. It is God felt as a pure Wind of Reason and also as something beyond reason. Kipling caught how it made sense of this world—'predestination in the stride o'yon connecting-rod'; but, being rooted in the Psalms, it also recognises the vastness of the desert's desolation. It makes an intellectual appreciation of the existential position and adds 'and yet . . .'

In my imaginary gallery at thirteen, Rupert and Napoleon were replaced by Montrose—the Calvinist who rejected the Theocracy; my Montrose was, and remains, unrepentantly Buchan's. Any consideration of Scottish history can still focus on the struggle between the two great Marquesses, Montrose and Argyle. (Add their contemporary Hamilton and you have St Andrew's House—'that's him that lost his head, folks said it wasna' a very guid ane, but, puir gentleman, it was a sair loss to him'—a fair description that of a decapitated bureaucracy and where the suffering would be felt.) The temptation is to go along with Argyle's gloomy logic. He offers the great bribe of the extremist: certainty. Montrose on the other hand had as his rarest quality his being able to feel passionately about moderation. Scott Fitzgerald recognised the mark of a first-class mind as the ability to hold two separate and opposed ideas in balance simultaneously. I reckon that passionate moderation passes the test. Montrose is an ideal Scotland of the mind. What of the visible reality in the early fifties?

'Every Scot is a Jacobite at heart,' said Lord Rosebery. On that basis I was a sentimental Nationalist. Yet this was a Nationalism, the Compton Mackenzie variety, that lost itself in emotion falling far short of action. It involved a glorification of the part played by Scots in building the British Empire. It made lists of Scottish Prime Ministers (Aberdeen, Gladstone, Balfour, Campbell-Bannerman, Bonar Law, Macdonald, and of course Asquith was MP for Fife, Churchill for Dundee. Wha's like us?) and Generals and it celebrated the great feats of the Scots regiments in the British Army. A Nationalism that finds its apotheosis in Lady Butler's painting of the charge of the Scots Greys is not going to take you far politically.

Outside my imagination, I was, and long remained, quite ignorant of Scotland; in important respects of course I still am, but then I had a geographical ignorance that was formidable. As a child I had spent some weeks in Aberdeen. In 1953 seven days in Edinburgh. Otherwise I was eighteen before sleeping a night in a city. I hadn't been to Glasgow or anywhere in the West. It wasn't either as if I had travelled elsewhere, except in imagination and even that moved more in time than space. I didn't cross the border till 1956 when I made a foray into a nineteenth-century past, attempting to win a History Scholarship to Merton College,

68

Oxford—city of spires to me, haunted by bells and rooks, I managed not to see the traffic. Very confined: when I first read Eliot the line that stuck came from his little poem on Glencoe, 'where the patient stag breeds for the rifle'; not perhaps the line of his that carries the fullest characteristic weight.

At thirteen I committed myself to the United Kingdom by going to Glenalmond. I was unaware of the symbolism of the act. It never occurred to me then or for the next five years that Glenalmond was anything but a Scottish school. I was even able to read of its foundation without the slightest uneasiness. Why should I be uneasy? Nothing was more certain than the United Kingdom. (A little later I even considered I might one day settle in Kenya and that shows I knew the stars had been stopped.) The Scottish Public Schools have often enough and justifiably been seen as an alien element—the fifth column of England. Since the aristocracy in the early nineteenth century had accepted anglicisation and were already flocking to Eton, Harrow, Winchester and possibly Rugby, it became necessary to provide at home comparable institutions for the sons of their professional men-of-business and the lesser gentry, so that some social contact might be maintained. This sociological interpretation is true. It misses however the degree of nineteenth-century commitment to the imperial idea and the United Kingdom; in the fruition of the Empire the characteristic ideology was centripetal. Natural enough. It is human to pursue success and shun failure. Separatism in the Victorian noonday was a crank's game, suited only to the despised Irish. The Scottish Public Schools—Fettes, Loretto, Glenalmond, Merchiston —were not an indigenous growth. They were planted, like colonies. But they took root. Outsiders might resent them. Those educated at the older city schools might condemn them as alien, apart from the Scottish tradition. They didn't feel that way to those within the community. We were sufficiently intense at Murrayfield. The few English were treated with a hostility that strove to be off-hand and contemptuous, but never quite managed it. (The Irish—without exception Orangemen or members of the decayed Protestant ascendancy of the South—were accepted). Perhaps we got it all wrong.

So, five years in a setting that might have been chosen by Cistercian monks, but was actually fixed on by Gladstone. Plato could hardly have asked for more control of those who were to be

Guardians. It ought to have moulded one, if the mould had still been true. But the Public School Code had never actually been formalised like Loyola's Spiritual Exercises. The British empirical tradition stemming from Locke and Hume saved us from that. Still the assumptions that informed the school ran deep, unrecognised then, unidentifiable till one had left many of them behind, like a little pile of clothes in the corner of a changing-room.

Criticism strikes backwards. The now sneers at the then. It is easy to wipe out the felt contemporary truth and substitute judgment. So much one is now ready to condemn obscures a happiness one remembers like something in an old diary, the record of another life. That says between thirteen and eighteen I was mostly happy. It attributes this happiness, which I believe in with the sort of credulity I give Gibbon not Proust, to a civilised tolerance that within limits prevailed, to friendship, to a willingness to respond that should be natural to youth and to the fun that acquiring knowledge is. Let the happiness then stand.

New figures appeared in the museum's gallery. Charles James Fox and Talleyrand were youth's pattern—the aristocratic man of pleasure who was also a civilised liberal man of power. (If like Fox or Mark Antony he was a loser too the reflection in the mirror was still clearer.) Fox reading Horace contentedly after losing thousands at faro; Talleyrand playing cards on the night of a coup d'état, hearing the guns, holding up his hand and saying, 'Listen, we are winning.' 'But who are we?' 'That I will tell you in the morning.'

Neither Fox nor Talleyrand was what the Public Schools aimed to produce. Then there was Byron and when I read that 'Don Juan' was a poem for disillusioned middle age, it became mine.

'Things will have to change if we want them to remain the way they are,' said Tancredo to the Prince in Lampedusa's *The Leopard*. A dominant class, and in the fifties the bourgeoisie was still the dominant class, always wants things to stay the way they are. Intelligent Conservatives recognise however that Tancredo's truth is not confined to Sicily. (Really intelligent Conservatives become Marxists; the best way to stop the Revolution is to make it.) Yet all the assumptions underlying our education rested on the conviction that somehow the world had stopped. Britain had won the war (we had a regular programme of Rank films in the gym on

70

Saturday nights to remind us); some rather regrettable, though perhaps necessary, re-ordering of society had taken place in its aftermath. That was now concluded. Churchill was back and would be succeeded by the Crown Prince Eden. It was a new Elizabethan age, conceived as a sunny afternoon. The nation was looking to its leaders. Us of course. First we would hold commissions during our National Service. That would give us practical leadership experience and would also accustom the masses to being led by us. It was good for them. They'd come to recognise it themselves. Meanwhile we mustn't forget we had duties, obligations, to those who didn't have our advantages. Once a term there was a Chapel collection for a Boys' Club in Glasgow. Once a term two of our chaps went down there on a visit. The Glasgow boys came up for a week-end in the summer. We were to that degree aware others lived differently.

This isn't the place to examine the validity of the leader concept. It would be better done by someone else also for it never quite took with me. I wasn't real officer material; something a bit suspect, even seditious, lurked within. I knew, and authority saw, that fundamentally I wasn't to be trusted. Yet one can't pass over the implications of a closed society existing in the 1950s on the assumptions valid before the Boer War, and there is something about Glenalmond that makes me think of the Boer War; perhaps authority recognised me as a pro-Boer, a consequence of being a Foxite. (What also casts doubt on the School's assumptions is this: it was a place you could read Galsworthy with approval.) One must at the least ask how far the poor performance of British industry in the last quarter-century has resulted from an educational system which allowed the nation to be divided into officers and other ranks. Bad enough in itself; partly responsible for the bolshiness of the other ranks, always ready, I'm told, like private soldiers everywhere, to skive. What however, of the equipment with which the officers were sent out into the world?

It was axiomatic first that the cleverest boys were destined for academic life, the professions or the administrative class. Lip-service was sometimes paid, at Saturday morning lectures, to the idea that they might be leaders in industry, but nothing in our education or in the ethos that enfolded us encouraged pursuit of the idea. Instead a system deliberately organised to produce Christian gentlemen who would run an empire continued to turn out those who were self-consciously gentlemen, nominally

71

Christian, but unhappily bereft of Empire. Deprivation. Yet for a long time one wasn't aware of it.

Only the stupidest boys, it was understood, would actually go into industry and help to make things. Even among them the first goal was Chartered Accountancy, and when I'm told that the accountants are everywhere taking over controlling positions on Company Boards I'm no longer surprised at how poorly so many companies perform. Below accountancy came the sales side; below that making things. Later, at Cambridge, I was to find this attitude still more frivolously reflected. There the media became the goal of many of the most intelligent. They even became actors.

Hard to pretend that our world-view was adequate; only possible if you kept your eyes shut. Not really such a difficult feat of course.

Suez should have opened them. But the most remarkable thing about Suez was the slowness of its effect. Even five years later intelligent students could be found to maintain we should have gone on. Impossible to be honest now about the motives behind my opposition to the adventure. I may have been spurred by disgust at the dishonesty of collusion or by the fact that Nye Bevan cracked a good joke about seduction; well anyway, my History master, rare at Glenalmond in being a *Manchester Guardian* reader, said it was a good joke. Conceivably I was prompted by school rather than by national politics. Actually it was natural that the meaning of Suez should be ignored, for Suez, far more than the Angry Young Men, knocked the props from under the Establishment. It was the last feeble splutter of country-house politics. We didn't at Glenalmond aspire to country-house politics, we belonged rather to the class that nodded approvingly at them.

If our political education was a poor preparation for the world outside, it's hardly surprising that many of us found we had no sexual know-how at all. 'I came out not knowing even how to speak to a girl,' said an Old Glenalmond encountered recently, 'let alone anything else . . .' (He has learned since.) Again we were, unconsciously no doubt, being prepared for a vanished world—where the women were months away by P & O liner, where you didn't marry till you could support a family and where there was always a club to retreat to. (I pondered deeply those days which London club I would join; used to study the list in *Whitaker's* appraisingly. Some days it was the Savile; others my brilliance would carry me into Whites.) In the Victorian age one-sex schools were not only defensible; they were justified. Men were training for a world without women; where they could live without making the accommodations that women demand.

There were no women in the imaginary museum that approximated to anything real; merely disturbing shapes.

The vice popularly associated with public schools was hardly in evidence at Glenalmond. Proust maintained that there was no homosexuality in Ancient Greece. This wasn't absurd. He meant that none of the mental attitudes connected with homosexuality in contemporary France were to be found there. Therefore what any reader understood by the word didn't in fact exist in Athens. The same might be said of the Public Schools. Such homosexual feeling as existed was quite different from the normal connotations of the word. Largely emotional, even truly Platonic, it was a would-be aristocratic sentiment fitted to an immature warrior caste—Pathans, Dorians, Public Schoolboys. Not surprisingly it often focused on scrum-halves. It wasn't fundamentally important except that again it didn't belong to the world of Admass; and it could hardly have been further from being gay.

There were of course credits. It would be blind to ignore them. If you can stand five years living at close quarters with your contemporaries you should learn blithely to ignore the opinions of all but the few you respect. We learned to be our own judges.

A pause on that sentence: we learned to be our own judges. Was it really like that? We could learn to be our own judges but we judged by standards we didn't invent for ourselves. That is the true rub. Anyone can pass his judgment with credit if he himself makes the rules. To accept a code and test yourself against it and not public opinion is another matter. It means being yourself while acknowledging the rights to existence and the value of other selves.

I never read *Stalky and Co* till I went to Cambridge, and of course the school depicted there was preposterous and nasty. Even by the Cam though I could acknowledge its rightness. I could assent to the virtues celebrated by Kipling even if elements within were ashamed of my assent. I don't greatly care for these elements now.

The aspects of self one most respects are often those invisible to others. This makes expression of that respect seem insincere or comical.

I never dream of Glenalmond and never recapture it without the conscious intellectual effort that cannot re-create it. There was something inorganic about the buildings; one was always aware they had been planted there. It was an idea imposed on a landscape.

In all this what of Scotland? 'We're a' Jock Tamson's bairns' is the title given to this book, but little enough of that feeling penetrated our morally cushioned though physically tough existence. I revert here to the idea of the centripetal fifties. It was not yet fashionable to proclaim that small was beautiful. You couldn't be a success except at the centre and that meant London, Oxford and Cambridge. There are simple local explanations. A majority of the senior staff was English. (Did they feel themselves missionaries in a barbarian land? To some extent.) They were themselves graduates of Oxford or Cambridge. I can think of only three masters in my time who came from other universities, and one of them was a Rugby international. And Oxford and Cambridge were acknowledged to be the top; they should therefore be our aim. The effect of this was to reinforce Johnson's observations about the fairest prospect open to a Scotchman. Its truth couldn't be denied. It would have been regarded as the height of provincialism to look elsewhere. Accordingly, there was never any question of a Scottish university unless you had first failed to get into Oxford or Cambridge. Nothing shows more clearly how Scotland was regarded as a home for the second-rate than this assumption that the best should seek their future outwith it. Pride in the Scot who had gone forth and prospered was permitted; as long as you remembered he would have been a bloody fool to stay at home.

If you set up to produce leaders you will be judged by the leaders you produce. On that basis the post-war claims of the Public Schools look shaky. The claims of the Scottish ones are ropier still; they can't even produce Tory MP's.

Autobiography shades into opinion that the boy himself could not have held. This makes of his life a retrospective exhibition where he doesn't recognise the paintings that are said to be his work. It doesn't ask what he wanted to do and where he wanted to go and it identifies choices and decisions he wasn't aware of taking. Try therefore another angle. Try the biographical.

There were two Scottish writers who held positions of unusual authority; unusual in that it didn't go with work of a sort one might expect to convey that authority. They can exemplify some of the stresses in our culture. They are of course Buchan and Mackenzie.

Buchan was the most Scottish writer—indeed *Vir Scotticissimus*. Mackenzie could have been American, was in fact part English and elected to be Scottish. On one level, an unpleasant one, Buchan was the Scotchman on the make satirised by Ford in *Some Do Not*. That was superficial though. He was really more complicated than this face he showed Edwardian England. Like his hero Montrose he was a Romantic Conservative, passionately moderate. His other heroes were Caesar who restored order at the expense of a liberty more fairly called licence, and Cromwell. Buchan's heart and sense of reverence inclined him to the Royalist side in the Civil war; his reason and style inclined him to Cromwell and made him appreciative of his greatness. Buchan's conservatism rested in his awareness of man's unmatched capacity for evil. His most formidable novel, *Witch Wood*, centres on the choice of evil in the name of good. In his thrillers he commands our belief by animadverting to the extreme fragility of civilisation. His heroes are aware it has been built with difficulty and can be wrecked with ease; his villains are men driven on by their lonely sense of I.

Buchan's life led him away from Scotland. His roots were in Tweeddale, in Fife and in Glasgow. He travelled by way of Oxford, London and South Africa to Canada where, as Governor-General, he represented the King and where in his last novel, *Sick Heart River*, he repeated again the doctrine he had learned of Challenge. There are no privileges and no rights except those you have earned. The work is its own reward. It was often said with a sneer that Buchan overvalued worldly success. Success however was not the reward; it was no more than evidence. Buchan pinned his political hopes on the Empire and the Anglo-Saxon races, and died in 1940 without being forced to lose faith. This was the ephemeral part of his message. It is a misreading to see Buchan merely as a bastion of the existing order; for him that order must perpetually justify itself. Buchan, aware of the evil in man, of the impish destructive side of his nature, was a moralist. He would have agreed with Scott Fitzgerald when at the end of his life Fitzgerald wrote that he was going back to character; cleverness wasn't enough.

Mackenzie was a lightweight by comparison. He never brought

75

his great natural talents together in a satisfactory novel because he couldn't take anyone but himself seriously and was yet reluctant to examine himself closely. Mackenzie, the professional, wrote to the end like an amateur; Buchan, the amateur, like a professional —there is always a concentration on the work in hand. As Buchan moved physically away from Scotland, Mackenzie, the Cockney, returned. He took up a position as the Grand Old Man of Scottish letters, but he might just as easily have settled in Wales or Ireland and one can't feel he would have written very differently. He tried to concentrate himself in an ambitious novel, *The Four Winds of Love*. It was highly praised by Edmund Wilson but one can't help thinking he mistook intention for execution. For, in effect, we have nothing but the usual self-indulgent charm and humour. There is a ridiculous hero, John Ogilvie, who dashes about Europe and the British Isles, madly loving women and small nations indiscriminately. He is a popular playwright, one of the best-intentioned asses in twentieth-century fiction, and Mackenzie takes him quite seriously. It's an extraordinary performance. Mackenzie cannot go any deeper because he has so completely rejected Original Sin (although a Catholic convert) and is so committed to Liberal values. Even his indignation is sentimental and selective—witness his treatment of the Black and Tans and the IRA.

Mackenzie returned to Scotland and became a founder member of the SNP. Buchan held to the end to his central belief in the Empire.

My education seems to have been an uneasy attempt to harness Buchan's politics to Mackenzie's morality. I'd prefer the synthesis to have been made the other way round. Buchan's politics are deader than New Zealand lamb—they've even been thrown out of cold storage. Africa red from Egypt to the Cape has a different meaning now. His morality however is something we might try to recapture; farmers are among the few who still respond to challenge which may explain why they seem one of the surviving healthy elements in society. And we must not blind ourselves to the mischievous nature of man. The impulse to create has to struggle against the impulse to wreck that our cities bear witness to.

We seem to be heading for something my education taught me was an absurd fantasy; an independent Scotland. It may not come about; the most common political error is to imagine that current trends must continue. Nevertheless it's near enough reality to make nonsense of much that was inculcated in me. Near enough to encourage a stock-taking. I would suggest we need more Buchan and less Mackenzie, more awareness and less sentiment. Scotland was always a hard country to govern till James VI discovered it could be done with a pen from London. Any football fan too will tell you how Scotland loves to dash the hopes she's raised. Now there is an alarming atmosphere of expectation in some quarters. When it's disappointed—as expectations from government usually are—we could be in for something unpleasant. We have forgotten that we have to make our own individual lives; manna and quails will be provided on Calton Hill. Perhaps. And we've forgotten too that swans drown ducks, for pleasure; because they want to.

BILL BRYDEN

'Member 'At?

---

1. When they bombed the distillery, when my native streets flowed whisky for the only time, I was at the breast down in the air-raid shelter. Or, so they told me.
'I fought the war for hooligans like you!' So they told me later.

2. The Fever-Van. Women at the closemouth in turbans, as they were called, with metal curlers underneath.
' Where is it?'
'Top flat.'
'It's terrible.'
I rushed upstairs to my house on the top flat. As I turned the corner . . .' 'cuse me, son,' said the Fever-man, in his Bovril-coloured uniform. There was my brother, happed in a red blanket, in the stretcher descending to the fever-van.
My mother crying. 'Dip-theria,' she whispered to Mrs Fox. 'Joey Fox! Joey Fox!' seemed to scream the budgie next door. 'Shut up, Joey. What are we gonnae tell 'im?'
I knew. The fever-van is the hearse for children. Sometimes. He didn't die. I still have a brother. Works for the I.B.M. Hardly see him now.
What you don't know then is that you travel. Carnegie, Graham Bell, doctors, lawyers, rivetters.

3. It was always called the Ranch. 'The Central Picture House'. Magic! Honest. Johnny Mack Brown (with Raymond Hatton), Hopalong Cassidy (with Andy Clyde), Lash Larue (with Smiley Burnette), The Durango Kid (my favourite), the heroes of Republic and Monogram. Sometimes it was better. Sometimes it was John Wayne. What you don't know then is that it's John Ford.
My Granny used to take me. 'Don't tell your mother.' And in short pants and 'sannies' we walked to the Ranch. There was a

fire inside to keep the queue warm and Paddy and Albert chucked you out when you talked back to the film stars. I suppose some of you wanted to be bus-drivers and train-drivers when you grew up. No way. A cowboy for me. But you knew you couldn't. You knew that everybody worked in the shipyard.

4. 'Pasha Only'
'member 'at?

5. School was good. Well. Aye. School was good. Except when you were late and got the strap. It's only later you find that in other countries they didn't give you the strap. At least, not for being late. They shouldn't do that. Far be it from me to deprive Lochgelly of its cottage industry but it's not on. I mean your wrists get blue and swell up and you start to cry, not from the pain but the injustice, and you think as you look at your swelling blue wrist that you're turning into Boris Karloff. No, it's not on. I didn't get the strap that much. I was bright and with the stutter as well the teachers' consciences probably got the better of them.

A lot of the boys got the strap a lot, but. Especially the ones with the Parish boots and the shaven heads. The 'Nurse' did that. Nits. They might as well have cut one of their ears off or tattooed numbers on. They were the 'poor' boys. They got the strap most. How were they ever expected to live that down? They shouldn't do that. It's not on.

6. 'Scoooot-laaaand! 'Scoooooot-laaaaand!'
'Goin' tae the game?'
' Wembley?'
'Aye'
'Hello!'
'Cowan's Wembley'. 'The three one game'. Apart from that and the day Jim Baxter became immortal, the rest were like funerals.

Raymond Glendenning on the radio. Jimmy Cowan putting the shutters up. 'And it's Matthews, Mannion . . . and it's Mortensen and he's through and it's a goal! England have scored. No, it's saved. Who *is* this man Cowan? Where does he come from?'

'Greenock, ya stupit bastard (excuse language). Morton player,' screamed my grandfather at the wireless. 'We're gonnae win the day,' he said quietly pouring the last sensation of Springbank

79

whisky he had bought in Campbeltown on his holidays and saved, just in case this was the day.

Why do we always expect to lose? Eh? Eh?

7. 'John Galt. Novelist'.

In the old cemetery, just down the road from the West Station, an announcement announcing the star tombstone. 'John Galt. Novelist: Buried here'.

A novelist? Frae Greenock? What did he *work* at?

8. When did we first find out about the Catholics?

'He's a Roman Catholic,' says the Protestant in polite conversation. Their church seemed pretty similar to our church but it turned out not to be a church but 'the chapel'. Their minister was a priest. Oh, they were different all right. Utterly.

'He's got red hair. It's obvious.'

'What school did you go tae?' asked the Protestant boy as he danced cheek to cheek with the 'smasher'.

'St Columba's,' said the girl. The boy took his cheek from her cheek.

I found this such unbelievable crap that I ended up in a mixed marriage. She's got red hair. Sometimes I think they were right.

9. Holidays in Campbeltown. Auntie Tina, Anna, Jamie, Bunty Paterson. The sea. Waves. Being sick on the boat. 1949. Three hundred Greenockians spewing their rings up beyond Lochranza. But, 'Arrived safely. Weather fine. Wish you were here'. The mystery tour.

'Is it Clachan or Carradale?'

'Cannae tell ye.'

'Is it Clachan or Carradale?'

'It's a mystery.'

'Look! I went on "the mystery" on Monday night and that was Clachan. I went on "the mystery" last night and that was Clachan as well. But, see Mrs Fielding! She went on "the mystery" on Tuesday and that was Carradale so I want tae know where "the mystery's" goin' the night?'

'It wouldnae be a mystery then, would it?'

'O.K. Tell me it's no' goin' tae Clachan. I hate Clachan. Full o' midges.'

'Look, are you comin' or no?'

'Och, passes the night.'

The driver at that moment changed the solution to the mystery and took her to Clachan just for spite.

How can I go back to Campbeltown? I want to take my children. I probably won't. I'm sure it's too . . . changed.

10. If you have a stutter people think you're daft. Is that true everywhere? Pity.

11. In front of me the school photograph Hillend Place School. The bell in the background. The teachers. Many dead. The pupils. Many caulkers, riveters, hauders-on, some draughtsmen, some Canadians, some Australians and me in the theatre.

'It's better than workin', I suppose.'

'Absolutely.'

When we left the big school I put in for film director. Charlie Cooke, the friend who has given me most art, most pleasure, put in for 'footballer, sir'. The Careers Officer, who I'm sure in his own time put in for something totally different, now knew better and smiled. I can still remember that arrogance. I got the 'Journalist' folder and Charlie got 'Architect'. Some of my best friends are journalists. There's even one who's a journalist on the *Architect's Review* or whatever it's called but who needs Careers Officers? They're out of date these days anyway. Outside the window, right now, able-bodied boys can't get work. Don't romanticise to them about the hungry thirties. You know how much records cost and clothes and haircuts and the pictures?

'The Ranch' is a furniture shop now. The 'BB's' a bingo hall and 'the King's' is shut.

The boy with the dyed hair outside my window needs a job. Any folder acceptable!

12. The Conservative came to my grandfather's door.

'I'm Mr Turpie. Your Conservative Candidate.'

'Sorry, son. We vote Labour like everybody else. You can have a cup o' tea if ye like.'

The Conservative came in. Had tea.

'You're wastin' yer time,' said my grandfather.

But where did that get him? 'Vote Labour'. Daubed on Gorbals walls. Where did it get anybody?

Jimmy Reid. What are *you* doing? What the hell am *I* doing?

81

13. I missed the Army. Remember the National Service? That was when some people went to Oswestry or Caterham or Munster for two years and came back ten years older.

Having missed the Army I have never been called 'Jock' or 'Porridge' or 'Haggis'. I'm glad I missed the Army.

14. When I was young there was a ball. And the ladies wore long dresses with tartan sashes and the gentlemen wore funny velvet jackets with diamond-shaped silver buttons, a lace hankie at their throat, leather 'sannies', the kilt (natch) and tartan hose-tops with a dagger stuck down the side. Is that what a Scotsman looks like? I found out later when I was the busiest best man on the West Coast wedding circuit that you could hire all that stuff. It came in a flat brown case from Keogh and Savage and since no knickers were included you had to presume that it was true what they say about Scotsman. I hate country dancing but I always wear the tammy at Wembley. We're daft. The whole lot o' us.

15. Helen Lees I loved. From a distance, you understand. Half a mile behind her walking round the Murdison Dam. I didn't speak to her, of course. Anyway, there was this other bloke and he was eighteen. What chance did I have. She came from 'the Port' and she was a smasher. I was daft. I should have taken her to Rossini's for hot peas or, maybe a raspberry ice if it was summertime. It wasn't just the stammer. We were all a bit shy about things like that. I've heard since it's all John Knox's fault but the truth is we just wanted to play football. I was even going to request a record for her on 'Children's Choice' but they wouldn't have played Bill Haley. It was always Roy Rogers and Trigger singing 'My Four Legged Friend' or that nyaff bloke with the small guitar singing about the owl and the pussycat.

I danced with her once. Nothing happened. I was scared I would stutter so I was very cool and said nothing. I tried to smile but my lips were stuck together. Anytime I did speak to anybody at the dancing it was usually something about the ability of the band or the texture of the floor.

Anyway, Helen. I loved you. I hope you're happy. Don't worry. You missed nothing.

Have you travelled or have you joined the SNP?

'He's all talk and no football. Know what I mean?'
The Scots are all football and no talk.

16. The Coronation. One TV in Carwood Street. Jean Chambers. Number seven. The whole street for the whole day in a two room and kitchen. The fireworks at the end. A Duke of Norfolk production.
'It was like V. E. Night.'
'Aye. She was lovely.'
'We must get one.'
'Sixty poun's a lotta money.'
'You can rent it frae Clydesdale.'
'Can ye?'
'Sure.'
'Fourteen inch?'
'Aye. It's that cheery. And there's Muffin the Mule for the weans.'
The first night we got the television Leslie Mitchell exploded and no amount of banging brought him back to Alexandra Palace. My father who was rarely furious near did his nut.
'member 'at?

17. I still went to church then. We sang the Psalms. Crimond. The Auld Hundred. The minister made us famous. My first television was 'Songs of Praise'. Voice broken. A second tenor no less. You don't stammer when you sing. Sunday school prizes. *Coral Island*. You always got *Coral Island*. One day I'll read it. It's bound to be better than *Biggles Hunts Big Game*. English rubbish.
It's odd, though, how superstitious church-going Christians are.
'You don't live in number thirteen do you?'
'Green. You're always wearing green.' Of course, there's prejudice there too. I still don't walk under ladders. Not if I can help it. If I really have to I pray, briefly. Is that prayer? Yes it is. Eyes tight shut as we were as children in the hard, dark polished pew.
I still go to church sometimes. Weddings and funerals and to pray. It's not talking to myself, is it? It's strange that in churches from Buenos Aires to Connemara no matter how decorative, how beautiful, how different, real church is Cartsburn on the hill above the shipyard down the street from St Laurence's where the Catholics used to go.
My father was an Elder. He didn't hate Catholics. He didn't
83

hate anybody except fanatics . . . Hitler, the Masons. He was a good man. When Paddy said his prayers, his rosary in his hand, in the upstairs room kneeling before my father's coffin, the Old Firm game at Ne'erday didn't make sense. I suppose Belfast's worse.

Church had the Sunday school picnic. That took place on the summer Saturday with the highest rainfall. We invented indoor sprinting on the station platform or under the covered bit of the pier.

The church had the Boys Brigade camp. That took place on the summer fortnight with the highest rainfall. Thunder stopped the tent building and by evening you're wondering why thirty boys are sleeping on straw in a cold church hall in Lamlash. You couldn't say you were homesick, of course, but Scutari's no fun.

I never joined the church. By that time I had discovered Sartre and Kerouac and Allen Ginsberg and Faulkner and it was fashionable to have doubts.

18. There was no feeling of being Scots. I was from Greenock and that was different even from being from 'the Port' or Gourock or Glasgow. Glasgow was 'the city'. When you went for your holiday in Campbeltown, the girls would whisper 'strangers' as you passed by. You were sophisticated. Rich even. A Scotsman was a man in a kilt. A teuchter from the Highlands or Islands. Skye was as far away as Bali. Except at New Year. Then you knew that no other nation carried on like that except maybe the Yanks, Canadians or Australians and they were Scots anyway. Hogmanay. First footing all night for miles in dazzling snow after 'the bells'.

'Happy New Year'.

A strange house. A welcome on the door and a dram. An old woman brought us in. We'd be, what? Well. Teenagers. Gave us a dram and black bun and shortbread and tea. Tea with your whisky, always. Nowadays she'd be frightened to open the door in case we mugged her.

Drunkmen. One word. Drunkmen. Usually carrying a box of 'Roses' as a peace offering to the wife. 'Hey, son? Hey, you? Can you tell me where my sister lives?'

Hogmanay. We knew we were the people then and the odd time we beat England at Wembley.

'See 'at wummen there? That is the *greatest* woman in the

84

world. Your mother. The greatest friend you'll ever have. God. *Bless* ye, darlin'. Awra best.' *My* father didn't drink. Ginger wine that my mother made. Teetotal. All Scots aren't pissed, you see? He always wanted me to stop drinking and get my hair cut.

The yard gates slowly opened and a thousand hangovers entered dreading the noise of the rivet hammers and even the whistle for the end of the shift.

I miss the New Year. It's not the same anywhere else. People think you're a Scotsman so at midnight they give you a bottle of whisky and leave you to it. They don't know it's 'the comp'ny'.

At New Year I wouldn't change my nationality for the last page of an Oil Sheik's bank book. Honest.

19. I liked the 'big' school too. Except the art class. I love paintings now. But then it was sitting with your pencil at arm's length, because that's what the teacher did, trying to draw a cube and a cone against a curve. I knew there was a catch. Only one of us managed it. He's a designer in the television. Lot of good it did him.

But 'Trigger's' English class was great. Shakespeare aloud and the plays of Sean O'Casey. Plays about people like us. Poorer than us. But people like us. And great titles *The Shadow of a Gunman, Juno and the Paycock* and, my favourite, *The Plough and the Stars*. Nobody found out who Picasso was or Calder or Klee but I found out from 'Trigger' about Sean O'Casey.

I got thirty-seven for maths.

French was good with 'Pop' Urie. I remember he wept. Just reading a poem by Prévert. He wept.

'Rappelle-toi Bar-bara?'

We all thought he had a fancy woman in Paris. I thought he might have been in the Resistance during the war and gave Barbara one before she was tortured by the Boche.

There was none of that really. His daughters were in my class. He just liked poetry.

'Wee Pat', the gym teacher, was a Greek. He was so fond of giving people the strap that I thought *he* was the man that tortured 'Pop' Urie's French girl friend!

'Te souviens-tu?'

We had to enter the school sports. The mile was the main event. I led the field for the first hundred yards and then chucked it. Later, however, I became a harrier and found out about stamina.

85

'Runner's Superb Finish', the *Telegraph* said. No kidding. Training's a mug's game.

We had 'Biddie' Byers for German. *Das Buch der Jugend* was the text. It was a yellow cover with a bad drawing of a Hitler youth and a Hitler youth-ess on the front. All the stories ended *Wir lachen laut!* I *hadn't* discovered Wedekind or Brecht then so I objected very strongly to learning it at all. I think that's one of the reasons I don't speak it fluently. 'Biddie' Byers is the other.

We always thought 'Biddie' had a wig but no one would have chosen an 'Irish' like that. Not even 'Biddie'. We had to act the stories out. They were mostly about camping and everybody wore short pants. By this time I had created the part of St John in a church play, so led by me the rest of the class had to act out these outdoor fascist tales, for 'Biddie'. We ate sausages, camped, yodelled, camped, went on holiday to the Schwarzwald and generally *lachend laut!* 'The Barrel's' class was worse for German. He took us when 'Biddie' was ill once and the stammer was on that day especially when I discovered that 'Biddie' said *'Ich'* and 'the Barrel' said *'Isch'* and 'the Barrel' insisted he was right. He had heard about my dramatic talent from 'Biddie' and, despite my vulgar accent, I had to lead the class back to the Schwarzwald in our gallegastins as we brought the pages of *Das Buch der Jugend* to life. Latin was terrible. The teachers were bored but one of them took us for 'Bible'. He was weird. He would read the good book to us and every time 'the Lord' was mentioned he called him 'Ya-Wee'. From then on he was known as 'Big Ya-Wee'.

'Wee Goliath' was the history teacher. He had to stand up on a chair to give Knight the strap. Knight was in my class but he was a man. You know? Grown up. We were still boys. I always thought that Knight fancied Helen Lees.

The geography teacher was so boring he didn't merit a nickname. There was nothing particular about him except that he lost his temper one day when he insisted that spaghetti wasn't grown on trees after we had seen it hanging from the branches the night before on television.

I also got thirty-seven for science. No wonder. The teacher ate chalk. Some of us got our 'Highers'. Some of us went to the university. Miracles.

20. You can't make a living in the theatre so you have to get a proper job. Interview time. I couldn't afford to train as a

chartered accountant because they don't pay you in chartered accountants' offices in shipyard towns. Think yourself lucky you don't have to dirty your hands. I became the Apprentice Public Health Inspector in the Royal Burgh of Port Glasgow. I enjoyed it. I could have been quite good at it. My boss, Mr Anderson, is still a friend. I hope.

And Bobby Grange who taught me all I know about choked drains, grease traps, faeces, infectious diseases, building inspection and the difference between ice cream and milk ices. I liked him too. When I left his class to go into the theatre his last words were: 'With your looks you could have been chief of Glasgow!'

21. So you end up a typical Scotsman. Prejudiced, Christian (when it suits you), well-educated, nostalgic, nationalistic, willing to travel, pro-Irish (well *they're* in the same boat), aggressive, proud, single-minded, occasionally pissed, occasionally singing, not mean (as a nation we are rather generous, you'll find), willing to accept second place too often, expecting to lose, easily embarrassed, passionate and football daft, standing there, thousands of us, in Wembley Stadium at the game. England 5 Scotland 1. A nation mourns.

'member 'at?

'SO ENDETH THIS CHRONICLE . . . WHEN ONE WRITES ABOUT GROWN PEOPLE HE KNOWS EXACTLY WHERE TO STOP . . . BUT WHEN HE WRITES OF JUVENILES, HE MUST STOP WHERE BEST HE CAN.'

Mark Twain

JOHN HERDMAN

Scots to the Backbone

When I was six years old I was given as a present a child's history of Scotland, H. E. Marshall's *Scotland's Story*. It was a companion volume to a history of England entitled, characteristically, *Our Island Story*; and it contained the sentences which follow:

> The hatred between England and Scotland has long ago died out. The two countries are now united into one kingdom, under one King. And every one knows that it is best for Scotland and best for England that it should be so. Wallace in his life did his very best to prevent that union. Yet both Englishmen and Scotsmen will ever remember him as a hero, for they know that, in preventing Edward from conquering Scotland, he did a good work for the great empire to which we belong. If Scotland had been joined to England in the days of Edward, it would have been as a conquered country, and the union could never have been true and friendly. When hundreds of years later the two countries did join, it was not because one conquered the other, but because each of the two free nations, living side by side, wished it. Thus the union became firm and unbreakable, and all Britons may honour the name of Wallace for the part he had in making it so.

At the age of six, of course, I did not see the interest and significance in that passage that I see today. To look back at one's childhood in terms of any specific context, such as that of national environment, is inevitably from one point of view to distort or even falsify it—to falsify the experience as it was lived then. It may be true of most feelings and apprehensions, on the other hand, that they have little real or substantial life until they have been thought, talked or written about. Certainly influences and determinants are no less real for having been submerged, ignored or misunderstood. To focus attention on a 'Scottish childhood' may

88

be attended with many pitfalls, not the least of which lies in the fact that to dissociate the purely personal from what may be of more general social interest is not entirely possible; but there seem to be enough, and sufficiently interesting, points of connection between the two to make the attempt worth undertaking.

I started by drawing attention to the passage quoted above because it seems to me to express very well, in its tortuous double-think, the central ambivalence towards Scottish nationality and Scottish experience which is characteristic of the social class into which I was born and in which I was raised. The prejudices and insecurities implied in such a posture appear to me to be far more deeply rooted and of more widely-ranging social impact than those arising from Calvinistic religious attitudes, which I believe to have been greatly over-stressed as a source of Scottish social and psychic tensions, certainly as regards recent history.

Edinburgh, where I was born and spent all my formative years, has for long boasted a particularly strong, coherent and well-defined business and professional upper middle class. My own people, on both sides of the family, gravitated there in the latter half of the nineteenth century, having been gradually increasing in prosperity within a rural environment for several generations. Though there were professional people scattered among the family —lawyers, ministers and so on—my immediate forebears were all businessmen, my father and his father before him being engaged in the grain trade in Leith, while my mother's people were tea and coffee merchants there. Their social attitudes were formed in the heyday of the British Empire—my father, born in the first year of this century, was always proud of being a Victorian—and on it, and consequently on the English connection, they instinctively felt their prosperity and their social position to depend. At the same time, particularly in my grandparents' generation, they remained close to their local roots, and the process of anglicisation lagged behind the achievement of prominent social status. My paternal grandfather, though he was the son of a well-to-do farmer, went to the local high school: but he sent his own sons, after Edinburgh Academy, to an English 'public' school. He was said to have been 'quite Scotch' (I never knew him), and to have made use of a fairly wide Scots vocabulary. A progressive and rapid anglicisation of accent over three generations in a social group which has remained very stable is easily observable. A Scottish accent is still considered acceptable in English social circles where an English provincial accent would not be, because it is still widely believed there that even upper class Scots employ one. This has long ceased to be the case.

My family exhibited a marked clannishness which I was very aware of in my childhood. Relatives might be criticised, disapproved of, or even disliked, but they were never disregarded or forgotten. There was a high awareness both of the ramifications of family history, kept alive particularly by the stories and reminiscences of old aunts, and of current developments. It has always seemed to me that most Scots of all social classes have a greater degree of such awareness than have most English people; I have often been amazed by the lack of interest in, or knowledge of, even their immediate antecedents exhibited by many of the latter. Our family awareness was undoubtedly to a large extent a function of social cohesiveness. A few black sheep in the family acted as a safety valve, and a kind of tolerant if slightly amused respect could be accorded to one or two who had distinguished themselves in slightly unorthodox ways, like the eccentric great-aunt on my mother's side who was a leading suffragette, went to London and became one of the first women to be called to the English bar. But it was as well if such examples were not found *too* close to home.

I remember from an early age hearing about relations and friends of the family who were 'down South'. England was invariably referred to in this way, and never by its name. To have called England England would have been to acknowledge it as a different country, and the friends and loved ones there as in some way cut off and separated from home. But they weren't, of course, they were just 'down South'. (It is precisely on such fears and weaknesses that politicians play nowadays when they tell the Scots that they (the Scots) 'don't want separation'.) While everyone I knew was very proud of being Scottish, they were also inordinately scared of being considered Scottish by the English; because the English were supposed to regard the Scots as in some way barbarous and uncivilised—'with heather growing out of our ears', in fact. To the English, therefore, it was necessary for the Scots to appear as English as possible; anything else would, in effect, be a betrayal of Scotland. A certain amount of defensive criticism of the English was however permissible, and particularly of the English in Scotland. The favourite comment was that they talked too loudly, and expended a great many words in saying very little. In hotels and restaurants there was frequent disparaging reference to 'loud English voices'—a phenomenon towards which I must admit to having retained an undiminished antipathy. Such criticisms were again, however, purely a safety-valve, releasing any recalcitrant antipathies or resentments before they could upset the delicate equilibrium of the neurotic system which controlled the consciousness of being Scottish and British at the same time.

I remember being aware of having this dual consciousness myself at quite an early age. I was interested in history, and for a long time my father used to take me every weekend to visit ancient monuments within range of Edinburgh; my awareness of being Scottish, which was quite fierce, was bound up with this historical interest. At the same time I had the quite consciously registered idea that England was 'more important' than Scotland; I was immensely lucky to be British, but there was the feeling that this was a privilege only extended by favour to a Scotsman. So the feeling of being, as a Scot, inferior *vis-à-vis* England, was compensated for by that of being, as a Briton, superior to everyone else in the world; and I was quite aware of this duality of attitude in myself.

The most confusing aspect of the ambivalent attitudes towards things Scottish which I breathed in from the surrounding atmosphere lay in the fact that the words 'Scottish' or, often, 'Scotch', were frequently used by my elders as terms of social disparagement. To be noticeably 'Scotch' in speech or behaviour was a mark of social inferiority. How was it that the same people who spoke of their nationality in such a way could at the same time be fiercely proud of being Scottish? Yet a gathering at our house after a Rugby international, for instance, would leave no doubt that this could be so. Besides, there were certain virtues, such as thrift, which were always being lauded in terms which suggested that they owed their value precisely to their being in some way peculiarly Scottish. 'I'm Scotch enough to hate waste,' my father often used to say. Again, although in general 'broad' speech was supposed to be 'common', there were plenty of 'good Scots words' which it appeared to be an admirable thing to employ, words like thole and stour and thrawn and girn; and there was always great contempt for BBC announcers who were unable to cope with Scottish place-names. Moreover the virtues of Scottish working-class culture would often be appreciated and praised within certain contexts, and were not seen as alien. There was no sense of the patronising in the laughter with which my family greeted the 'Scotch comics' at the annual Christmas pantomime, for instance. In many ways our responses were compartmentalised: different, even diametrically opposed, responses to the same realities seemed appropriate within varying contexts.

A much repeated family story which I first heard when I was very young concerned an uncle of mine who, at the age of about four, was asked by an American lady in a London hotel, 'Are you English, little boy?'—to which he stolidly replied, 'No, I'm Scots to the backbone!' It was a sentiment which, for all the diehard Unionism of my family, won him unstinting approbation.

Awareness of the geographical diversity of Scotland was sharply awakened on our family holidays, usually spent in Speyside, Perthshire or Argyll. These were ritual institutions, though diminished since the days of my parents' childhood, when the custom had always been to take a house for 'the whole of August'. (I still have relatives living who believe that it is unwise to travel on August 1 because of the exceptionally heavy traffic—irrespective of the day of the week on which it happens to fall.) In that era they would book entire railway carriages and pack trunkloads of every conceivable household effect, and still find room for bicycles, dogs and servants. These bourgeois holidaymakers acquired, I am sure, a more intimate knowledge of the places they visited than most landlords, absentee or otherwise, possessed. In general they did not, like the aristocracy, come mainly to shoot and fish, though in later generations they took more to these diversions. The main pursuits were walking, bicycling and picnicking, and these remained the staple holiday occupations in my family throughout my childhood. Most of the favourite haunts had family nicknames, acquired decades before, which were probably corruptions of Gaelic names —the Benny and Molly burns, for instance. There is a hill in the Cairngorms shaped like a sugar-loaf, by the western approach to the Lairig Ghru, called Carn Eilrig. In our family, though, it was always called something that sounded like 'Ca-nochan Teucher': my grandfather, it seems, had invariably called it that, but nobody could remember why, or what the name might mean. It was only when I came to learn a little elementary Gaelic that I realised that what was meant was *Cnoc an t-Siucar*, Sugar Hill. My grandfather must have known the area well when it was still Gaelic-speaking.

One of the conditions which made our kind of Highland holiday possible lay in the fact that general access to the wide open spaces was still limited, more or less, to 'people like ourselves'. We demanded for our picnics a degree of solitude which today would be virtually impossible to attain, except perhaps in midwinter. If we were not picnicking at one of our accustomed haunts it was difficult enough to find a spot which was acceptable to everyone at the same time; and once we were installed our enjoyment was often diminished by apprehension at the possible invasion of the place by other people. If a head was sighted round half a dozen bends of a burn five hundred yards away there was constant tension from the possibility of its nearer approach; and often a mournful cry of 'People! People!' from the leader as we approached a potential site turned us on our heels to trudge back with rugs and picnic-baskets the way we had come. If we were staying in a hotel, of course, the proximity of other human beings had to be reluctantly accepted, and this was compensated for to some extent by the rich opportunities presented for critical observation, often of a sociological cast. A favourite pastime at meals was the identification of 'penholders'—those who held their knives like a pen, instead of with the handle properly tucked away in the centre of the palm. We never, of course, acknowledged such a stricture as arising from anything so simple as snobbery. A justification might run: 'It's so impractical, how can they possibly get any *purchase* like that?' Another feature of hotel holidays was the wealth of nicknames rapidly acquired by our fellow guests: 'Obscene Shorts', 'The Hairstretcher', 'The Coarse Runt'. I was always mortified by the thought that someone else in the hotel might have coined a nickname for me.

Inordinate shyness and unease with people in general made me steer clear of my contemporaries as much as possible, and thus indirectly had the effect of alienating me, from my earliest years, from my social environment. At school, of course, people could not be escaped, but I tried to avoid like the plague (though not always successfully) the social functions in which I was expected to participate, like children's parties and, in adolescent years, private or charity dances. My appreciation of the Christmas holidays was customarily vitiated by the dread of having to attend parties, and I was for ever hoping against hope that I would turn up on the wrong day, in spite of the embarrassment which would naturally be entailed: a day late, of course, and not early, otherwise the whole ordeal would have to be faced anew. On one occasion I did actually somehow contrive to appear a day late, and felt, perhaps correctly, that I must have used up my store of good luck for the rest of my life.

Where I did benefit culturally from my background was in the easy access which I had to the books in my parents' house. The backbone of this collection consisted of the traditional Victorian library inherited from my grandparents' day, with its full sets of Dickens, Scott, Stevenson and other nineteenth-century novelists, histories, travel books, theological works, Romantic poetry, and a row of useful and informative leather-bound prize books won by my maternal grandfather at school (one of them was Smiles's *Self-Help*). The acquisitions made by my parents, a high proportion of which were detective novels of the twenties and thirties, interested me less, though I did revel in Sherlock Holmes and, less discriminatingly, in Bulldog Drummond. My parents encouraged my interest in books, and also in music, as desirable peripheral adjuncts of a respectable life, suitable for someone of a studious and intellectual disposition; but as it turned out these led directly into concerns which became central to me and which were destined to frustrate my parents' hopes for the sort of future which they envisaged for me. Throughout my childhood I myself had two parallel visions of my own future, the respectable, realistic one of becoming a lawyer or an advocate, and the private daydream, far-fetched but dear to my heart, of a career as a composer or a writer. I have no recollection, however, of being troubled by any acute conflict between these alternative scenarios, for they occupied quite separate areas of my consciousness.

My formal education was of course entirely directed towards the encouragement of the first possibility. Far more than religion, education is the matrix in which are gathered all the social priorities, attitudes and assumptions of the Scottish *haute-bourgeoisie*. (The role of Church in my childhood, though by no means unimportant, was almost entirely a matter of convention. The attitude of my parents' generation to such matters as sexual morality was already determined far more by social constraints than by those of traditional belief; though I am sure that this would have been much less true of the previous generation.) The most indispensable information to have about anyone consisted of the facts of how and where they had been educated; and of course the English private system—the public school and its preparatory adjuncts (whether or not the schools in question happened to be located in Scotland was immaterial)—represented the peak of the hierarchical pyramid, and indeed the only fully acceptable educational proposition. It would never for an instant have occurred to my parents that to educate me in any other way could conceivably have been in my best interests. Knowledge of the state system and how it worked was so hazy as to be almost non-existent; my father until the end of his life invariably referred to state schools as 'the board schools', and believed intransigently that the term 'secondary school' referred to inferiority of status in relation to the private system. Any attempt to persuade him of its actual meaning would be dismissed with the words, 'Well, I can assure you that it never *used* to mean that!'—so self-evidently appropriate appeared to him the meaning which he had assigned to it.

The first two years of my education, from the age of four, were spent in the mixed nursery department of a private girls' school, and were to provide me with my only experience of co-education. Had I been aware of that at the time I might have appreciated this spell more keenly. It was followed by five years as a day-boy at a preparatory school in Edinburgh, then two as a boarder at a similar school in St Andrews. The former was an eccentric establishment with an atmosphere which seems to me in retrospect to have had something almost Victorian about it. Detecting signs of scholastic promise in me, they pushed me on so fast that by the time I was nine I was in a class whose average age was eleven, a formidable discrepancy at that stage in a child's development. The result was that I lost a great deal of grounding and came to regard maths, for which I had little aptitude, as a system of black magic, to cope with which the only expedient was prayer.

The St Andrews school taught me well, and the lack of constraints during leisure hours there allowed for weekends roaming the town and countryside on foot or bike, and some of those times I remember with pleasure. On the other hand discipline was so lax that the boys, left more or less to their own devices during their generous allotments of spare time, spent much of it tormenting each other, both mentally and physically. I was not sorry to leave.

Because I had not taken kindly to boarding-school life it was decided that I should go not to my father's old school in Yorkshire but to a public school in Edinburgh—though of course still as a boarder. It is hard to say what, if any, difference it would have made to my development had I gone to the English school. The school I went to probably had in general a more Scottish ethos than any similar school in the country, and counted among its inmates a fair admixture of such earthy Scottish types as Border farmers' sons. Yet so far as classroom time devoted to the study of Scottish history or literature was concerned, the school might as well have been in Middlesex as in Edinburgh.

Athletic pursuits were of course held in very high esteem, and the discipline more than made up for the shortcomings in that direction of my previous school. You could be beaten by the prefects for (for instance) walking through a door in front of them or being twice late into bed—which might mean by ten seconds. Prefectorial beatings for a senior pupil could entail, if my memory serves me aright, a maximum of a dozen strokes of the tawse on the right hand and ten on the left. (I am told that things have since changed.) These prefects were fond of saying that the school was built on privilege, and to underline that point they allowed you to put your hands in your pockets after you had been there a year, open one button of your blazer after two and a second after three; but the middle one remained as tightly sealed as a chastity belt unless you attained prefectorial rank. The people who operated this system, masters and pupils alike, were of course no more monstrous by nature than anybody else, and indeed I have pleasant and happy memories of many of them. They merely manifested their shortcomings, as the majority of people do, in terms of in-herited and acquired class and cultural attitudes. The education itself, apart from its complete lack of any Scottish dimension, was very sound indeed, and not nearly so narrow in the upper forms as in some such schools.

During my five years at public school I subscribed entirely to the accepted, predetermined image of the future which had been envisaged for me. Indeed, I was able by this time to look upon the forms and traditions of my own social background with just enough detachment to see in them a certain attraction and even romance; but not yet with sufficient objectivity to contemplate any break with them. I quite fancied to myself the dignified and highly formalised life-style of an Edinburgh advocate. I still have some of my school essays, which reveal an entirely conventional and unimaginative adolescent, reproducing with a fair amount of skill the attitudes currently being implanted in him. Though I wrote spontaneously between the ages of six and twelve I stopped entirely in my teens, and did not start again until I was at university. Verse-making for the annual poetry prize was a mere formal exercise. Literature never so far as I can remember impinged upon my consciousness in any real way during those years; I looked upon it in the same light as I regarded any other school subject, though I probably enjoyed it more than most. That it could have any vital bearing on my own life never occurred to me. Not that I would ever dream of blaming those who taught me for this: the sense of the subtle and shifting relationship between art and life is not something which can be taught; it is apprehended intuitively if at all, and in its own good time.

Although I was unhappy at school and dislike the system under which I was educated, I cannot say that I regret the experience. I suppose that it is impossible for anyone to regret anything which has gone to make them what they are. That need not imply self-satisfaction, or anything other than a lack of desire to be someone else, or an inability to contemplate such a possibility. I cannot consider the question of whether I would prefer to be the person (or any one of the infinitely extendable series of possible persons) I would have been had I been educated differently. Nor would I waste any energy rushing around trying to get the system abolished. Any oppression or injustice involved in it is really so minimal compared with what the world has to offer in that respect, and the way of life it serves is so moribund, that its existence can be tolerated as a contribution to sheer variety, and tholed if necessary to keep the equality mongers occupied with something to campaign against. The only way I can express an objective view of my education is by saying that I would never for an instant consider subjecting any child of mine to a similar process. Not however because of a supposed injustice to anyone else, but because of the injustice to him.

It was tacitly agreed at school that Oxbridge was the highest and most appropriate goal for any promising pupil to aim at, and an arts degree at Cambridge followed by Law at Edinburgh seemed a natural approach to my intended career. After school, however, I spent a rather mixed year, partly attending lectures at Edinburgh University while I completed the work for a Cambridge scholarship, partly working in my uncle's office in Leith, and partly travelling in Europe; and during that year I began to change a good deal. My father saw the changes coming, and they worried him. I have always thought of my father as a man who was never entirely at home in the circumstances of life in which he found himself, who often lost patience with his own kind; perhaps because, in spite of having a strongly gregarious side to his nature, he was at the root a solitary and individualistic person, like myself. I often wondered whether the strength of his opposition to my decision to become a writer, my conversion to Scottish Nationalism, and the concomitant departures from the established life-style of our class, owed something to a suppressed personal hankering after such apostasies. 'What the father kept silent,' wrote Nietzsche, 'the son speaks out; and I often found the son the father's revealed secret.'

Until I was eighteen I had never been out of Scotland for more than a week; and when I went up to Cambridge a year later I had spent more time in Europe than I had in England. My upbringing and education had led me to expect to find in Cambridge a natural extension of my previous experience; to my astonishment I found it a quite alien cultural world. The process of reorientation towards that previous experience began for me there and then.

DONALD CAMPBELL

Four Figures in a Personal Landscape

One: The Old Man

I was born in a little house on a quiet street, on the outer edge of a quiet town in what is, very possibly, the quietest county in Scotland. Not that it was physically quiet, of course. The county of Caithness is almost totally flat and the town of Wick is on its coast, so there were times when it seemed that the house would be shaken from its foundations by a wind that came roaring in from the loud and almost humanly-angry sea. Apart from that, there was a war on at the time, which meant that there was always the chance that an odd bomb might fall during the night.

The first friend that I ever had lived next door. He was an old man, a retired fisherman called (rather appropriately) Peter. On most fine days, Peter was to be found sitting at his front door, mending nets—and, often enough in those days, I was to be found sitting right beside him. I'd be about four years old at the time and wanted to become a fisherman more than anything else in the world. So I'd prattle away about boats and catches and how fishermen had to be brave and strong and ready for all kinds of weather, while Peter would smile and nod and occasionally murmur a word or two in encouragement.

I think it was this encouragement that really attracted me to him. He was prepared to take me seriously (at least, it seemed as if he was) and that was more than anyone else was prepared to do. I was convinced of this by virtue of one particular thing that he did—he used to call me 'boy'. Now, in Caithness—at least, in the Caithness that I knew as a child—four-year old male specimens of *homo sapiens* were rarely addressed as anything other than 'boyagie'. 'Boy' was a term of affection restricted to peers, an expression that one man used when talking to another. Although he was old and retired from the sea, Peter fulfilled all the require-

99

ments of my heroic image of a fisherman—I can see him now in his gansey and his sea-boots, his cloth cap perched on the back of his balding head—and to be called 'boy' by such a man made me feel as if I were as good as he was.

Sometimes, when he felt like talking—or, more than likely, when he'd become bored with all my chatter about fishing—he'd tell me stories. Peter's stories were never concerned with personal reminiscence—at the time, these would have bored me—but were mostly pieces of legend that he'd picked up here and there throughout his life. Sometimes, they were concerned with Scottish history —I discovered those, years later, in Scott's *Tales of a Grandfather*—and sometimes they had to do with Caithness and the sea. Of those, I forget all but one, a story about the old, ruined castle that lay some way down the coast from us—a place universally referred to as 'The Old Man'.

The Old Man—or Oldwick Castle, to give it its proper name— was probably built in the tenth century by one of the Norse Earls of Caithness. When I asked Peter about it, however, he laughed and told me the old rhyme.

'The Old Man of Wick was a very old man
When the Old Man of Hoy was a boy.'

Then Peter told me about Sweyn. Many years ago, it seemed, the Vikings had come to Caithness, thrown out the savages who were living there, and started to put the place to rights. Sweyn's father had been one of those Vikings and Sweyn himself had been born in Staxigoe. When he had grown to manhood, Sweyn had naturally gone to sea to become a fisherman. One night, when he was away fishing in the Pentland Firth, some bad Vikings had come down from Orkney, murdered his father and mother and all the rest of his family, and burned down the house.

Understandably enough, this made Sweyn very angry. He got together a party of his friends and they all set off for Orkney to take their revenge. When they reached the stronghold of the bad Vikings, they found them eating and drinking and having a high old time. Their leader was sitting at the head of a long table, with all his cronies around him. This didn't worry Sweyn, however. He just walked straight up to the man, took out his axe and hit him over the head with it. That was the end of the bad Viking leader.

100

After that, Sweyn gave up the fishing and became a pirate. He sailed all over Britain, raiding and plundering and building up a huge store of treasure. In fact, he amassed such a pile of treasure that he didn't know what to do with it all—so he built The Old Man to be his storehouse. To make sure that his treasure would be safe while he was away on his raiding, he had built the storehouse on a rocky outcrop, separated from the main part of the cliffs by several yards, so that thieves would find it difficult to reach. That was why The Old Man was such a dangerous place that I was sure to get into trouble if I ever went near it on my own.

As Sweyn grew older, he became angrier and fiercer. He travelled further and further afield in search of new places to plunder. It seemed that his thirst for more and more treasure would never be satisfied, until at last, in Ireland, one of his enemies surprised him in his sleep and put him to death. That was the end of Sweyn, but The Old Man was standing yet. As for the treasure, nobody knew what had happened to that.

Peter has been dead these many years. Until quite recently, though, The Old Man stood on its lofty rocky plinth, as permanent and indomitable as ever, ready to outlast as many centuries as it had already seen. The Local Authority, however, had other ideas. With the cold and unsentimental logic that all Local Authorities seem to have these days, they decided—very properly, I'm sure—that the place had become altogether too dangerous and would have to come down. Sweyn's precautions, so effective against the heroic villains of his own time, proved useless when faced by the villainous heroes of today. So The Old Man is no more.

When I grew up and took a deeper interest in the history of my people, I remembered Peter's story about Sweyn and tried to check it out. Although I found that, apart from a few errors of fact, the history of Sweyn himself was real enough, I could find nothing to connect him with The Old Man. Still, I don't suppose that matters very much. Even if it wasn't true, it was a good tale—good enough, at least, for an old man to tell, on a sunny afternoon, to a little boy who had no one else to play with.

Two: The Boy

The boy's name was Les and he was—and still is—the toughest human being that I have ever known. At the end of the Second

World War, my father, an Edinburgh man, returned home and started to pick up the threads of peacetime life. My mother and I naturally joined him, and I left Caithness, for good, when I was five years old, and came to live in Edinburgh. It was there that I first met Les.

I ought to say, at this point, that the Edinburgh in which Les and I grew up was not at all the Edinburgh of popular legend. This was no gracious Festival city of cultured stone, pan-loaf speech and stand-offish manners—I only knew that such a place existed when I grew up and read about it in the writing of spiteful Glaswegians. In my eyes, accustomed as they were to the open fields and big sky of Caithness, Edinburgh seemed a dark, dirty, noisy and smelly conglomeration of grey, canyon-like tenements, with thousands of people living in burrow-like communities within them. Everything—the streets, the houses, the shops, the faces and the clothes of the people—seemed to be covered in a kind of greyish dust, the sound of the traffic thundered in my ears all day long, and the smell of nearby factories—manufacturing yeast, glue and rubber—almost made me physically sick. We lived in a room and kitchen on the top-flat of a tenement in Downfield Place—so much smaller than the four rooms, garret and lean-to shed of my grandmother's house in Wick—and, to begin with at least, I suppose I was rather unhappy.

Les lived across the street and he didn't do anything to make me feel happier. I have one, enduring picture of him in my mind; dressed in a suit of grey corduroy, he is standing in a group of other children, bouncing up and down with exuberant glee. This was a habit that he had when he was happy, a habit which was the main reason for his nickname of 'Bounce'. He was the natural leader of the kids in our street and he laid down the law with an iron fist.

I first fell foul of Les when we went to school. I suppose there were a number of reasons for this, but the one that sticks in my mind had to do with the way I spoke. When I first came to Edinburgh, I had a thick Caithness accent and used many dialect expressions which were unfamiliar to Edinburgh ears. At the best of times, this led to great confusion in my life. I remember one occasion, for instance, when I went into a sweet shop and asked for 'a lockie o black sugar', by which I meant that I required a small quantity of liquorice or (as an Edinburgh boy would have said) a 'daud o sugarolly'. The shopkeeper hadn't a clue of what

I was talking about and it was only after the passage of many misunderstandings that I was able to get what I wanted.

Children being what they are, my accent became a source of great hilarity to my schoolmates. When they asked me where I came from, and I answered 'Weeck', they were totally bewildered until they found out that I meant 'Wick' and then they would erupt in gales of laughter at my seeming inability to pronounce the name of the town correctly. In addition to this, the Caithness dialect involves a fairly frequent use of the diminutive—I'd talk of a 'bookie' when I meant 'book' and 'lassockie' when I meant 'lassie'—and, to the Edinburgh sensibility, this not only sounds quaint—it sounds soft. At that time, I had had very little experience of other children and not the least idea of how to stick up for myself. So I let them laugh and did nothing about it. As far as Les was concerned, that meant that I was a cissy and therefore fair game for a battering.

And Les battered me. He seemed to batter me every day—so often, in fact, that I seemed to spend most of my life thinking up ways to avoid being battered. I remember one, very intricate plan that I made; I would get myself a hammer and lie in wait for Les in his stair. When he came in, I would wait until he passed me—the stair being dark, I counted on him not noticing my presence—then I'd leap upon him from behind and hit him over the head with the hammer, hurting him badly enough to keep him off school for a very long time. Fortunately for Les (and myself!) I never quite got up the courage to carry out this plan—and the batterings continued.

Eventually, however, the inevitable happened. Les battered me once too often. I can't remember the exact occasion when I turned around and battered him—but I know that it happened, because, ever since that day, I have never allowed anyone to laugh at me with impunity. Moreover, my experience with Les stood me in good stead on the occasions when I returned to Caithness on holiday. By this time, I had acquired the Edinburgh accent that is my normal mode of speech today and, although I could—and, to some extent still can—speak Caithness when I wanted to, the local kids took rapid note of this and tried to apply a similar persecution. Having survived the Terror of Downfield Place, however, I was in a good position to ensure that there was no repetition of my Edinburgh experience and, whoever was on the receiving end in any batterings, it wasn't me.

103

After I battered Les, he stopped being my enemy and became my friend. Just how good a friend he could be was proved a number of years later. By that time, my parents had moved from Downfield Place to Ogilvie Terrace, a pleasant little street on the edge of Harrison Park. We weren't all that far away from the old district, however, and one afternoon, Les and another boy came over to visit me. My mother gave us tea, then I took my two friends out to show them round my new district. A local butcher who lived nearby had a garden which contained a large number of apple trees and, boys being boys, we decided to help ourselves. Unfortunately, we were seen and I was recognised. Before it was time for Les and the other boy to go home, the police were at the door and we were all in hot water.

As I was, in a manner of speaking, the host, and since I was the one who had been recognised, I suppose it looked as if I was the one who was in the most trouble. I remember to this day how astounded I was when Les, in the most matter-of-fact manner, stepped forward and bluntly told the policeman that I wasn't to blame, the whole thing had been his idea, and I'd only become involved by virtue of the fact that I was with him. This was a complete lie, of course—they'd never have known about the apples if it hadn't been for me—and it didn't get any of us off the hook, but it was the most noble act of friendship that I have ever experienced.

Three: The Minister

I suppose the most important cultural influence of my childhood was the Church. For good or ill, the Church permanently affected my views on politics, history, drama, art, literature—everything, in fact, except religion.

When I say the Church, of course, I'm not talking about the building, or even the institution. I mean the congregation, the community of people who gathered together for worship every Sunday—and who stayed together for most of the rest of the week to do all sorts of other things. Boys Brigade, Boy Scouts, Youth Club, Bible Class, Dramatic Society, Badminton Club, Darts Team—you name it, the Church of Scotland has it in some shape or form. When my play *The Jesuit* (about the seventeenth-century Catholic martyr, John Oglivie) was first performed, the first question I was usually asked by anyone who came to see it was—what's

104

your religion? I made the mistake of telling one rather zealous newspaper reporter that I had been baptised in the Free Church of Scotland. This was duly reported and I've been branded ever since as a communicant of that austere and, in many ways, thoroughly admirable faith. I'm sorry to say that this just isn't true—although I was certainly baptised into the Free Church, I was brought up in the good old Church of Scotland, where religion occupies a poor third place behind the narrow concepts of social conformity and bourgeois respectability.

If that sounds disapproving, let me hasten to add that the fact that I hold this view in no way blinds me to the fact that many good men worship according to the teachings of our established Church. I need look no further in this respect than the example of my own father, who has discharged his duties as an ordained elder for almost thirty years, and who has always done his best to live his life within the precepts of Christian teachings. As I know from experience, there are a great many others like him.

The churchman who made the greatest impact on my life was a minister. A rather shy, scholarly, gentle and courageous man, the Reverend Dr David MacDougall taught me more about what is important in life than any man I have ever met. In point of fact, it is ironic to reflect that Dr MacDougall was so successful in convincing me of the importance of both spiritual and intellectual honesty that I was ultimately forced to reject the beliefs that he himself so intensely held. That being the case, I don't think he would have blamed me for it.

I first met Dr MacDougall at Dalry Church in Edinburgh—now called St Colm's—where he was the minister and where my father is still an elder. I suppose I must have been twelve or thirteen years of age when I first came under his influence, about the time that I entered his Bible Class. Even before that, however, he must inevitably have made an impression on me by virtue of his preaching.

Perhaps I ought to explain that the power of oratory is the quality that all Presbyterians value most highly in their ministers. I don't know if it is still the case that most Presbyterian ministers learn their sermons by heart before delivering them, but it was certainly true not all that long ago. At one time, in fact, even the practice of bringing notes into the pulpit was looked upon with deep disapproval, and any minister who did so was adjudged a 'bad preacher'—the most damning criticism any congregation can make of its pastor. I don't know how many times I've heard someone say, in criticism of some minister that 'he's a good enough man, I suppose, but a *terrible* preacher.' And I know of at least one case where a congregation were prepared to turn a blind eye to their minister's sins—which included, I might add, lechery and drunkenness, principally on the grounds that the man was an excellent preacher. The sermon is one of the few pieces of ritual that the Presbyterian churches allow and, in the case of the Church of Scotland at least, it is little else. Few people actually listen to what the minister *says*.

Dr MacDougall was a superb preacher. He had a rich, rolling voice that could either throb with compassion, whisper with reverence or roar with rage. In addition to this, he possessed, to a remarkable degree, a gift of projection, an ability to reach out and touch his congregation, not as individuals, but as a united whole. From the moment that he uttered the words 'Let us worship God', he created an occasion. Given this essentially dramatic sense, it mattered little that the subject-matter went a fairly considerable height over the heads of most of his congregation—it was the way that he said it that mattered.

In the Bible Class, away from the rituals of the pulpit, he was rather less effective. Here, he had to discard the role of preacher and take on the one of teacher—something that he wasn't very good at. He had little idea of how to interest young people and absolutely none of how to impose discipline. Since I think that he regarded the Bible Class as simply a chore that he was expected to perform, I don't think that this bothered him all that much. Certainly, he took no offence when, on one occasion, I took steps to correct the results of his shortcomings, thereby indirectly pointing them out to him.

Our Bible Class wasn't very large and numbered about fifteen. These included a couple of empty-headed, rather trivial girls who were in the habit of gossiping openly (and noisily) while Dr MacDougall was speaking. Following their example, most of the others began to do the same and, very soon, Dr MacDougall could be heard only through a perpetual buzz that was becoming louder and louder each week. Dr MacDougall himself seemed not to notice this, but I was becoming increasingly angry. Finally, I could stand it no more and one week, when it was my turn to take the collection, I used the fact that I was on my feet to deliver a strong lecture to the Bible Class. I told them that I was sick and tired of people taking the mickey out of the minister and, from then on, anyone who felt like talking when Dr MacDougall was speaking would answer to me. That shut them up.

I hardly realised at the time, of course, that I was, in effect, making a criticism of Dr MacDougall himself. Perhaps he didn't realise it either, because he merely smiled and thanked me and went on with the Bible Class.

As I was growing up, I came to know Dr MacDougall much better and learned a great deal from him. Most importantly, I think, he taught me how to treat the Bible as a *book*, rather than a piece of church furniture. He taught me how to place its teachings in a context that was religious, philosophical and historical in nature. Ecclesiastes, for instance, is a very Jewish book (Dr MacDougall was a leading Gentile authority on Jewish Studies) and can only really be read and understood by taking the history of the Jews and the tenets of their religion into account.

Dr MacDougall also taught me a great deal about literature. A rather enthusiastic lover of the classics, he taught me everything that I know about poetics and prosody, those areas of verse-making which, although despised in our schools today, are essential in the making of all good poetry. He encouraged me a great deal in my writing, acting as my sponsor for several years in the Moray Dairsie Medal Competition, which is an essay competition for young people which the Church of Scotland organises every year. He also encouraged me a lot in my reading, telling me once that I should never allow any text, however bad, to defeat me. This has proved an invaluable piece of advice, since my observance of it has developed in me a deep sense of structure, a quality that no good writer can be without.

Dr MacDougall always said that I ought to become a minister and it is one of the deepest regrets of my life that I was never able to oblige him. I was, however, able to fulfil at least one of his expectations for me. When I showed him my first gauche attempts at poems, he smiled and told me that they were really very bad. Then, much more seriously, he thought for a moment and looked me hard in the eye. 'However,' he continued, 'You *are*, very definitely, a poet.' Whatever my critics might think, write or say about *that* statement, I am convinced enough that I was right to keep on trying.

Four: The Girl

The girl had red hair, blue eyes, a trim figure, a lively personality and an exceptionally high intelligence. She also had a name, but I'm not going to reveal that because, apart from anything else, the girl herself was never really important to me. It was only the *idea* of her that I loved.

In the summer of 1956, when I was sixteen years old, I spent a holiday in Caithness for what was to be the last time in nearly twenty years. I was hardly aware at the time, of course, that this would be the case and, on my return to Edinburgh, I thought that I had my entire future mapped out fairly clearly. I would finish my education, take my Highers and (hopefully) go on to University, then get a job—either in teaching or journalism—somewhere in the North of Scotland. Without intending any disrespect to either my father or to my Edinburgh cousins, I continued to regard Caithness as my home and wanted to get back there as quickly as possible. It all seemed perfectly straightforward—and would have been, if I hadn't met the girl.

We met at school, an institution that I loathed and which taught me next to nothing. Basically, I suppose, this was because the prevailing ethos of the place placed a great deal of emphasis on the spirit of competition—and I have always been a distinctly non-competitive type. Furthermore, although I can see the value of competition in the fields of sport and entertainment, I feel that it is usually counter-productive—not to say immoral—when it comes to education. I believe too much in the pursuit of knowledge *for its own sake* to have much use for those—and there are a great many of them in Scotland—who would use learning merely as a tool for 'getting on'. 'Getting on', however, was the sole *raison d'être* of the school I attended as an adolescent and, although I was only dimly aware of it at the time, I resented it— and, because I resented it, I became alienated from it. I became a misfit.

Now, being a misfit when you are a grown man and a committed artist is not at all hard to bear and, in fact, can have its compensations. When you are a sixteen-year-old schoolboy, however, it is quite another matter. For all that I had decided to keep my cynicism to myself, play the game according to the rules of the Establishment and walk off with my certificates at the end of the course, this didn't prevent me from being unhappy. It wasn't

108

so much a case of life being unpleasant for *me*, as it was of life seeming to be so pleasant for *everyone else*. School was a distinct community in which I could find no identity and no place. There was an aching void within me that I felt for every minute of the day.

I met the girl in a rather unusual place—in a game of hockey. I rather fancied myself as a hockey-player at the time, and I was playing right back for the school boys' team against a team from the girls. I wasn't very good at hockey, but I did have one very effective trick that I used to play. When the ball came to me, I would deliberately hold on to it to draw the opposition attack—then, at the very last moment, I'd send a long, diagonal pass shooting up the left wing. The effect of this was to catch the opposition on the wrong foot and set up our own winger for a goal. It was a good trick—which, proved successful on more than one occasion—but, this time, it was altogether too good. The opposing winger came charging on to me just as I was about to hit the ball, and the end of my stick hit her in the mouth. I was extremely concerned—and said as much—but, as it turned out, she was perfectly all right and we were able to continue with the game.

This incident, however, played an important part in the forging of our relationship. Had it never taken place, I very much doubt if I'd have even have got up the courage to talk to her when we met at the School Dance that Christmas. It wasn't that I was a particularly shy boy—at least, no more than sixteen-year-olds usually are—but the fact was that she was the most scintillatingly attractive female creature that I had ever seen. Not only was she so attractive physically, but she had a certain quality that even the best-looking of the other girls lacked. It was a definite assurance, a poise, a confidence in herself as an individual. I was anything but confident but the incident on the hockey field gave me the opportunity that I needed. Not only did I talk to her, I danced with her for the rest of the evening and ended up walking her home. For the next seven months, hardly a day passed when she wasn't in my company—and not a single minute when she wasn't on my mind.

I often wonder why most of us pretend to make light of our adolescent love affairs—which are, after all, among the most significant relationships that we ever experience. In this case, it was a relationship which acted as an effective crossroads in my life

—my entire future was determined by it. Even if I do say so, with the wisdom of hindsight, this is no exaggeration—as I think that I realised even then. After I met the girl, the lack of identity that I had felt at school vanished overnight. For the entire duration of our relationship, I could, quite literally, do no wrong. Life took on an entirely new prospect; I was fulfilled, I was self-confident, I was happy for the first time in my life. I was so happy that I even enjoyed school and, had our relationship endured for even a few months longer, there's no telling what might have happened to me. One thing's for certain, though—the fact that our relationship didn't endure wrecked all the plans that I had made for my return to the North of Scotland. It wrecked them completely.

I am not saying that this was the girl's fault. As I said at the start of this section, it was never the girl *herself* that was important, but an idealised vision that I had of her. When that vision turned out to be human, I just couldn't take it. When our romance ended, it not only destroyed my plans, it nearly destroyed *me*. All of a sudden, I just didn't care about anything any more. I lost all ambition, all interest in a future that was anything more than humdrum survival—I even lost my desire to write. I suppose I took on a rather gigantic case of the sulks. But it wasn't the fact of her rejection that gave me the sulks, but what I believed to be the reason for it.

I suppose there were many reasons for the break-up when it came. As far as I was concerned, however, there was only one. The girl had told me that she wanted a career—she wanted to go into journalism, she said—but it eventually became apparent that what she really wanted was a husband. I had no quarrel with that—at the time, I'd have married her like a shot—but the fact was that I wasn't good enough for her. She gave me all sorts of reasons to sweeten the pill, of course, but that was the one that stuck out like a sore thumb.

This shattered me. I just couldn't believe it—I couldn't believe that someone that I had placed on such a high pedestal could be capable of acting out of such a crass motive! My life, up until that point, had hardly been a sparkling success, but no one had ever told me that I wasn't good enough. 'Remember when there were the bad guys and the good guys?' says Arthur Miller in one of his plays. I'd always thought of myself as one of the good guys, a hero—with the girl, naturally, as my heroine. Now, I found out, she wanted to be with the villains—it was as if Maid Marian

110

had turned Robin Hood over to the Sheriff of Nottingham.

As it happens, I was right about the girl not wanting a career. She never went into journalism and, not long afterwards, she married a guy who was at school with us. I believe that they've been very happy for the best part of the last twenty years. As for me, I learned two very important lessons from the experience, two of the hardest lessons that I have ever learned. The first one was that it can be extremely painful to try to make other people conform to an image that you have made of them—people are not cardboard characters who exist only for your convenience. Secondly, I learned that there are very few villains in this life—and no heroes at all.

Once you realise these things, of course, you may not have grown up but, at the very least, you are no longer a child.

LIZ LOCHHEAD

A Protestant Girlhood

I was born at the bleak end of 1947. Stafford Cripps' Age of Austerity, I know now. I remember, can I really remember, or is it just mythology—Power Cuts and Sweetie Rationing?

There were a lot of us born then, most of us to parents just as recently demobbed, just as newly optimistic and no better housed than my father and mother were. We were the Bulge. I knew that then, as we advanced from Primary School to Secondary School to Higher Education with a lot of fanfare and rhetoric from the newspapers. The Bulge. A single frame from a comic book, this gigantic Easter Egg a spotted snake had swallowed in the Dandy Annual—this was how I pictured it as we were squeezed through the gullet of the Education System stretching everything to breaking point.

We lived, my mother, my father and I, in a single upstairs room in my grandparents' house. My father's side. A big between-the-wars council five-apartment. Roughcast. Pebbledash. Six in the block. In the shadow of all the steelworks, Colvilles, Anderson Boyes, the Lanarkshire—number thirteen, the Broadway, Craigneuk, Wishaw. Whenever I heard on the radio the Lullaby of Broadway I thought they were singing about us.

The place was full of adoring grown-ups all easily charmed and exploited by a smartypants toddler. There was my Gran, my Grandad, my father's youngest unmarried sister and brother—my Auntie Jinnet who was engaged and my Uncle George who was Restless. He was considering emigrating to Corby with half the workforce of Anderson Boyes. My Grandad spent a lump of every afternoon lying on the bed under the top knitted blanket in the back bedroom, often with me burrowed in between him and the wall, prattling and pulling his hair. He had been a miner before the steelworks and he had a touch, more than a touch, of silicosis. His lungs weren't so good.

112

But he was good and loud in arguments. Round the tea-table I remember him, long before I could make head or tail of it, the arguing—especially on Sundays if the rest of the family were there, Bill and Jean who had two children and a prefab and Annie and John with my baby cousin. He had been a miner. He was a Unionist. He was angry at how his sons and daughters had come back from the Forces voting Labour. Said they'd sold old Churchill down the river. He blamed the war for a lot.

He had been a miner. He was a Unionist. In the early twenties, preying on fears aroused by the recent large influx of Irish Catholics to Glasgow and the industrial West of Scotland, the competition for jobs, the suspicions about cheap blackleg labour, the hard times a-coming, the Scottish Unionist Party successfully neatly split the working classes. I know that now. Divide And Rule. People have told me. Then I knew a father and his sons around a table. His white hair. My grandmother wheeshting and clucking. The words Catholic and Protestant. Raised voices.

He was not an Orangeman. He used to say he had nothing against anybody. He was a good churchgoer. Regular. He talked about Idolatry. And told me about Covenanters. There was a blue and white plate on the wall with a man-on-a-horse who was William of Orange. He was Dutch. Delft. They had brought it back from Holland when they had visited my Uncle Robert's Grave, my Gran and Grandad. After the war. He had been my father's second-youngest brother. He was dead. There was a picture of him in his uniform. I spent a lot of time looking at this photograph to see if there was anything different about a picture of somebody who was dead. It was easier with my Aunt Edith. She had died aged seven of measles ten years, fifteen years, a long time ago. It was possible to imagine, when I squinted at the family group with her in front, something slight and shifting and other-worldly about her sepia presence among her lumpier solid brothers and sisters. They said I'd her Eyes. My mother said nothing at the time, later up in the privacy of our own room said nothing of the sort. Mine were brown.

The room wasn't that big. There was my mother and father's big high bed. And my brown-varnished cot squashed in at the end of it. A green-top card table and chairs, big brown boxy rexine chairs. There was the radio, no, it was only a speaker really, it had one on-off switch, no tuner, it was attached to my Grandparents' radio downstairs. We had to listen to whatever they listened to,

113

when they switched it off we'd had it. We listened a lot though, plays, music-nights, Take It From Here. In April 1948 over the speaker they heard Stafford Cripps' Budget increase the price of cigarettes from two-and-four pence to three-and-four pence and my forty-a-day father looked at his sleeping or squalling four-month old daughter, said well that's that and gave up just like that, never smoked again. Another piece of family mythology.

There were few ornaments. My mother and father's engagement photo, framed. Head and shoulders, printed in monochrome then hand-tinted. Cherryblossom—brown hair, pink cheeks, carmine lips. A sweet smile each and a youthful look. And the wedding photograph. Full length. My father in his army uniform, my mother in the A.T.S. She said she could stand it, the Khaki, because she'd good colouring and anyway there just weren't the coupons. She'd had nothing else to fit her because the army food blew you up. She'd consoled herself with what the teacher had told her away back when she'd had to wear the brown fairy dress in 'Fairy-Leather-Apron' in the school concert—that brown eyes like that could bring out the beauty. She said the big excitement had been seeing if my father's leave got cancelled and the whole thing was off for the time being. It had been touch and go, she said. But she'd got a lot out of the A.T.S., enjoyed it, met all sorts. She said the main thing was not to marry too young. She recommended waiting until you were twenty-four like her. It had been the ideal age.

She talked to me a lot, did my mother. All day when my father was away at work. Bits of her life became legends. Descriptions of dance dresses, what devils they'd been she and her sisters, stories of how my Auntie Elsie, fifteen and with soot on her eyelashes, had brazenly stolen someone's officer. She says now I was great company as a kid. She was that bit plumper again than in the wedding photograph. Seems that every time something my grandmother said rankled her (it was my father's side remember) every time she had to just swallow it all or just start a row over some domestic division, every time they'd had yet another disappointment over some house they'd been after—she'd walk me in my go-chair, chewing in her misery a whole quarter of newly unrationed sweets.

For a while we tried the other set of grandparents. I don't suppose things were much happier or easier for my mother and father. They kept putting in for houses here and there, getting nowhere.

114

They didn't seem quite so deadly respectable, my Gran and Grandad Forrest. For instance he swore, up to the point of 'bloody' and 'wee bugger'. He had been in the Navy in the First World War, still sang songs my grandmother tutted at. He had a terrible voice. A groaner. Tone deaf. He sang me Sad Songs—'The Drunkard's Raggit Wean'—and laughed and tickled me when I got a lump in my throat. My mother always said what a right good storyteller he was, had a way with words, embroidered things just enough.

My grandmother said poems. Long storytelling poems. At sixteen she'd been maid to one of the Misses Reid who'd been an elocutionist. And gave lessons. My grandmother had remembered by heart every word, every inflection, every arch or pointed gesture of the voice. I grew wide-eyed at Little Orphan Annie (and the goblins will get you/too/if/you/don't/watch/out), tearful at the melodrama about the little girl searching for her dead mother (And I'se looking for heaven/but I can't find the stair).

I absolutely loved them both. But it's easy to love your grandparents.

When I was four we Got A House. A brand-new council four-apartment in the small mining village of Newarthill. A couple of miners' rows, the school, the pub, the Tallies' Café, the Post Office and the Co-operative. Now the pits were dying and they were building two schemes around it. It was four miles from Motherwell, expanding industry.

I went with my mother to do the place up before we moved in. I could feel her excitement. Eight years married and a house at last. We approached along newly laid out paths. What would soon be careful turfed lawns and neat rose-borders were great banks and churns of clay. The rooms seemed big and empty and hollow-sounding. Full of space. Cream plasterboard walls. My mother said they could get the downstairs done but maybe if she stippled the upstairs rooms there would be no need to afford to paper right away. She measured and scrubbed and I looked out of the window at the signs of life, a parked pram, the colour of someone's curtains, elsewhere windows whitened for privacy. A girl quite a lot bigger than me was wheeling a small girl in a pushchair and dragging a small boy by the hand. My mother said I should go and make friends, that was the beauty of it, I'd have lots of boys and girls to play with. It would be great for me.

I went out warily. I suppose it was my fault really, hit the wrong note, too bluff, too braggy. I told the girl my mum and dad had a new house and it was a Brand-New One. She said huh, who hasn't and asked was my dad a keyworker. I said he wasn't he worked in a big office in Glasgow and she said he *must* be because these were Key Workers' Houses. Or else somebody must have put in a good word for him with the Councillor.

That was what it was like, to be a child. The place, the people. Soon you went to school. You don't want to go back there, you've been padding it out with bits about your parents and so on. Why go back there anyway? You know how you hate it when you find yourself back there with no choice, in Dreams. And you're always running along the corridors, you're late and this is always the primary school and the corridors are spiked with pegs and coats with a damp doglike smell and you keep swinging through doors into classroom after clasroom looking for your class, your empty place. And can't find it. Or there's the dream where it's always the high school and the history class and suddenly there you are out in the middle of the floor wearing nothing but your vest. A too-short vest. You pull it down in front of you, then the back of you, don't know which way to turn. Everyone is laughing. And you don't know which part to expose.

So why try to tell it? Not for nostalgia. Not to say ah when we were wee. Not for all that merely. Easy, too easy to write a kind of proletarian Molesworth compleat with French-teachers-who-couldn't-keep-order. Yes, there were a lot of real-life cliché characters, you could without one word of a lie dredge up the Recognisable Particular. Something to have people smile to remember. Except that would not be honest enough, to thereby imply that it was any of it absolutely harmless. So go back, dig deep, but know that you'll not get at any of the things you accepted most easily, that hurt you the most. You will be the last person to know what they are.

Newarthill Primary School. A big black stone-built place with railings around it. Old, it had the date 1897 cut into the stone between the Boys Entrance and the entrance marked Girls. I was five. My mother took me to enrol and on the way back she said she hoped I'd stay on at school, go to University if I had it in me, she and my father would make every sacrifice. It was a great shame my father had never had the chance.

We were taught by Look and Say. Apple says ah. Miss Brown was not particularly pleased that I knew how to recite **Ay Bee See**

116

Dee and recognise the characters, said that Parents didn't know the damage they did. But I learned to read very quickly. Most of the class did. We learned by rote. Off by heart. Tables: nine sixes are fifty-four ten sixes are six-ty; Similes: as black as coal, as green as grass; Singulars and Plurals: hoof, hooves, sheep, sheep, fish, fish or fishes, spoonful, spoonsful. We chanted aloud like a prayer.

The school did seem to be staffed by a collection of remarkably similar mainly maiden ladies. The odd widow. Does my memory lie to me in showing me so many Miss Jean Brodies twenty years beyond their prime? Each time before you moved up a class you were afraid, had heard the shouting spill into the corridor, had heard the rumours of beltings for Nothing, knew that this was going to be the most terrifying class in the school. But it always turned out to be much the same. The teachers had their moods. The sums got harder.

Each day started off with the Lord's Prayer, half an hour or so of Bible. The Story of Joseph read verse each around the class, a chapter a day, missing out Chapter thirty-nine, being the spicy one where Potiphar's wife stages her seduction scene. But I was suspicious enough, had the sense to read it anyway. Or we had to repeat what we'd learned at home a verse a night, Isaiah 53, or the gibberish of a Scottish Paraphrase.

> 'Oh god of Be-ethel by hoosand
> thy pe-ople Still are fed
> Who through the Weary
> Wild-er-ness has stole our father's leg.'

After the Bible then Reading, your homework piece, without a stammer. Aloud. Then Spelling. Every night you had to learn one group from the little red and white Schonell's Essential Spelling Book. Every day we wrote them down.

see	six	by
tree	fix	cry
been	box	try
sky	sweet	fox

More than two wrong got the belt. Hugh Gilmour and Jeannie Nielson got the belt every day. For the Spelling and for other things. Remember his pink flush, his orange hair, his gallus grin, how cock of the walk he was when he swaggered back to his seat. He kept count of his beltings, his boast was that he could take it. Farm Jeannie Nielson was big and cow-dumb. Smelt of the byre, carried it in on her shoes. Her eyelashes were matted together with a sticky affliction called Sleep. She cried easy. Sat alone at the front to see the board. When one of us nice girls or clever boys was Bad we were moved down to sit beside her as punishment. She cried easy. Still she was belted for her Spelling Errors.

Can that be true? Can they have been so cruel, those dedicated ladies with their flowery smocks to keep the chalk-dust from their good-wool dresses, with their churchy peppermint mothball breaths. They all played a club-footed piano, taught songs. Flow gently Sweet Afton. On their autumn window-sills bulbs split their sides in purple crocks, in spring milky frogspawn quickened into wriggling punctuation marks. The weather chart was filled in up to date. They taught us to tell a tree by its leaves. Once, thanks to my teachers, I knew the difference between the Mute and the Bewick's Swan. Nature Study was the gentle ladies' favourite subject. Once for weeks we had a snuffling hedgehog in a cardboard box. They loved animals.

Everything was a competition.

Every Friday there was a reshuffle, you were moved in descending order from the back row to the front, according to your marks, according to your stars.

Every summer there was a week of Tests. From this was decided the list of prizewinners. *Black Beauty*—for General Excellence Elsie Lochhead has been awarded Third Prize (Equal) in Class Primary V says this florid label, laurel leaves, a garland. My mother thought this poor and to be honest I had not thought to sink so low. One place lower next year and it would be a mere Certificate of Merit. No book.

And there was the Gala Day to consider too. Newarthill Miners Welfare Association organised it. There was a marquee, the sweet smell of cut grass under canvas, a tombola, a ride around the village on the back of a crêpe-paper-decorated lorry, milk and a bag of buns. And every year from the Top Class of the Primary School there was the Gala Queen, the cleverest girl in all the school, not the prettiest, the most popular, not the voted-for. The miners respected education above all. Like everything else this was a glittering prize for cleverness, the true worth. No one questioned it. The Girl Dux, the Queen, and the Boy Dux her

118

Champion. Led around on a white horse. Made to wear brown velvet doublet and hose, usually wrinkled. And the Queen in a white dress in a car like a wedding car.

Even the colour of your sewing was a prize. Twice a week at the end of the afternoon for an hour we were Split Up. The boys from the girls. The boys got handwork, raffia mats, the girls sewing. We made lap bags of linen to keep our knitting in. Learned in theory to turn a heel. The linen was in three colours. Miss Ferguson gave the cleverest—according to last weeks Test Marks—first choice. Pink, blue or helio. No one liked helio. Miss Ferguson said the stupid did not deserve a choice in anything. Had to take what they got.

History and Geography. The Tulipfields of Holland. Bruce and the Spider. Or Composition. A Day In the Life of a Penny, A Walk In the Rain. Never use the word got or a preposition to end a sentence with. Mine were usually best, sometimes they even got Read Out and I'd be extra proud, go home with something good to tell. To maybe make up for the six out of ten for sums. I loved Composition. I knew what they wanted you to write. I knew to be one of the Winners, the Clever Ones, you had to be clean and neat and quiet and eager and just anxious enough under the tense time-counting pressure of Mental Arithmetic or Dictation. I loved school.

Except for that Worst Day. Remember it. Go back. Before your bath on Friday nights your mother combed your hair in her lap with a fine-tooth comb, carefully checking. There was once she found Something, said who had you been playing with, never never to try on anyone else's pixie. Next day she bought a bottle from the Chemists called Suleo Emulsion. Smelt horrible. A sticky pomade. You had to keep it on for at least forty-eight hours, so on Monday you had to go to school slicked with it, your hair in ratstails. You prayed the nit-nurse would not come that day. She did not come often, five times, six times in the seven years of Primary School. But that day she came. You could not believe it, you wanted to die, you wished you'd wake up and it wasn't true. Your class went to the hall. You queued up. Girls first. She lifted all your skirts quickly, tested your eyes, made you read a row of letters, looked in your ears, looked at your hair. You felt sick and dumb. She said Hmm, and stay behind please. The rest of the class went back to the classroom, looking back. Your best friend waved. You were left there with Jeannie Nielson and Hugh

Gilmour. The Nurse said did you realise you had a Dirty Head. You explained about your mother checking, the stuff she'd put on, on Saturday. She said Ah yes but this should have been noticed Before. But there was probably no need to notify the parents as it was being dealt with. She gave Jeannie Nielson and Hugh Gilmour a Letter to Take Home. You went back to the classroom, burning, heard whispers, kept your head down over your sums, tried to concentrate. You were in the Very Back Seat, were Top that week, all the morning heads kept turning round, the people who had been your friends hissing Did You Get A Note. You did not answer. Later you said you had really been kept back because you might need glasses.

My mother was angry when I told her at lunchtime. Said what had the nurse meant should have been noticed before, she checked every week in life. My grandmother was there on a visit, said it was a disgrace and if my mother did not go and see the headmaster then she would. I said please granny don't come, just leave it. It was a whisper.

All afternoon you dreaded it. Kept looking at the glass above the door waiting for her smart felt hat to show, for the rap of her knuckles. Eventually the headmaster came, asked to see you, took you to his office. Asked for the whole story. Your grandmother was on her high horse, saying it was a well-known fact they'd rather leave a Dirty Head for a clean one. The Nurse was there, flustered. The headmaster was saying the whole thing was Very Regrettable. You felt terrible.

It was a much worse day even than the Qualifying, which kept you awake for nights. We were the Bulge. There was a shortage of places. Competition would be that much greater.

You passed for Dalziel High, and a five-year Academic Course. The best. Your mother and father said they had always known you would.

We went for the uniform early on in the school holidays. A royal, black and white striped tie, two pale blue shirt blouses, a grey permaprest pleated skirt and a royal blue blazer with a school crest and a Latin motto. *Summa Petenda*. Seek the Highest. Almost every night for two months I tried on my uniform, admired it. I read school story after school story that summer, *The Chalet School, Mallory Towers*.

To be at Dalziel High is to realise that you are part of a tradition. So goes my schoolgirl round hand English Ink Exercise.

120

Thoughts After One Week As a New Dalzielian. An Essay. I get (scored out, replaced by *obtain*) a feeling of History although I do not understand it from the Greek writing around the Entrance hall outside Room One, and greatness from the gold names on boards that line the Assembly Hall. The School Duxes, The Intermediate Duxes, The School Captains, The Roll of Honour showing those who died in the war that we might be free. My ambition is to be worthy of this tradition.

I got a good mark. The English teacher said the best of them had been very good, very little to choose between them. But in my second Essay was the chance to shine. Was Top. My Favourite Season. Autumn. Compare the falling leaves to ballerinas pirouetting to the ground. Get in the words golden-ochre and russet. And not least of my pleasures when autumn spreads its golden wings around us is a good book and tea by the fire and toasted muffins and jam while the wind and rain blusters on the window pane: I don't think I'd ever tasted toasted muffins and jam in my life but they sounded right, English enough, almost Enid Blytonish. It was not a lie, exactly. Just that it had never occurred to me, nothing in my Education had ever led me to believe that anything among my own real life ordinary things had the right to be written down. What you wrote could not be the truth. It did not have the authority of the English things, the things in books. Muffins and jam. I knew what they wanted you to write. My grown-up writer's fear is that this might still be so.

It was a good school. They kept telling you so. It had wonderful playing fields, old traditions, an excellent academic record which it was up to you as One of the Lucky Ones to maintain. Perhaps to its credit it practised no discrimination between the sexes, rather we girls in our school ties were only slightly inferior boys. Its teachers were of the old school, tweedy old suits, chalky gowns, kept order mainly by a pedantic weary sarcasm, the occasional tawse. The school had a Debating Society, A Junior Choir, A Chess Club, A Christian Union. I wanted to be in everything. There was an annual Drama Festival with a play from every class in the school. (I can still remember my debut in 1.A.'s play, a fantasy by A. A. Milne: 'Oh, Oliver! Isn't it a *lovely* island.') And all the time around us sprawled gritty old Motherwell, its steelworks, smoke, pubs, Orange Halls, Gospel Halls, Chapels, Churches, social clubs, shops and factories.

We did Latin. Learned Grammar. Learned up pages of French

121

vocabulary, never spoke a word, translated in writing of course from French to English. History was a mish-mash of dates, the exam was a series of sentences from your history book with key words missing and, to show you'd learned it, you filled in the blanks. The History teacher had No Discipline. We played an elaborate game where you changed shoes with your neighbour, they changed them with the next person and so on round the class. When the bell rang there was a scramble of swapping back. Geography was marvellous. Logical. A Revelation. Position, Climate, Natural Vegetation. It seemed that maybe people were different because their conditions were different. Something which had never occurred to me in twelve years. I had thought God made everybody different and people were born that way.

Art was doing washes. Chrome yellow to palest lemon, crimson to blush rose. But I loved it. And yet English was my favourite. Shakespeare. The Merchant of Venice. His Jewish Gaberdine, the Quality of Mercy. Put it into your own words. And Poetry. Horatio On the Bridge. And how can man die better than facing fearful odds/for the ashes of his temple and the something of his gods.

Maths was the Hated Thing. Algebra was awful. I decided I could never understand it. Every evening my father tried to help me with it, it became our battleground for about two or three years until he gave up. I could not posibly be so stupid. I was determined I could.

Ungrateful, unfair to say only this of your father. Didn't he always encourage you? Yes. Took you to a planetarium, tried to get you interested. Brought home special paper glue when you wanted to make up that cut-out cardboard puppet theatre, never complained when you didn't use it, just left the top off, let it dry up. Took you to the baths. Bought you Bumpers once because you liked them so much, although your mother had said to get Clarks Sandals. Once when your wee sister was just a tiny baby, you must have been ten, he took you to Edinburgh for the day all by yourself. He took you to Art Galleries, remember the thrill of a *trompe l'oeil* picture of Mary Queen of Scots with a skull, a deathshead replacing her when you walked past at a slant. And a picture of a Minister on Skates, a black sober man on thin ice. You went to John Knox's house, up Scott Monument, into the Camera Obscura. And he took you out for lunch and let you choose what you wanted from the menu. You asked him what were rissoles and he said something sort of Italian and he didn't fancy

122

them but it was absolutely up to you. They were delicious.

All your childhood they told you this, at school, at home. Freedom. The Protestant Ethic and etcetera. One's own conscience face to face with god. Free will. Why then the guilt when what you have wanted has seemed to be different from what they wanted you to want?

That is how it was with Art. It was Art which caused the rift between you and your schooling. Before that the report cards glowed.

I was fifteen. I had chosen my course for the Highers, English and French, Geography, Latin and Greek. I had only just begun Greek. There were three of us in the class only, two of the cleverest pupils of the year, a pair who would go on and get in the First Hundred of the Bursary Comp. no bother. And me. I did not like to be bottom, even of three. I did not find Greek so congenial as Latin. One day from the bus I saw Jim Lindsay who had left school the year before. He was walking down Newarthill main street, he had a huge piece of hardboard under his arm. He looked free. He was at Art School.

I decided I wanted to go to Art School. I would drop this stupid Greek, do Higher Art.

It wasn't that easy. The Art teacher said yes if you've got permission from your parents and the Rector. My parents were not keen. But if that was what I wanted. The Rector said no, it would be a waste, said Higher Art was given absolutely no credit for University Entrance. I said I wanted to go to Art School, was sure, decided absolutely. He said I ought to do English at University and besides some of the people who had gone on to Art School had been awkward types, caused trouble, worn white socks, been lax about the uniform, thought they were somebody special.

After my third visit to his office he said all right, washed his hands of me, said it was my own look out.

In the Art class we got absolutely no instruction. But perfect peace to do what we wanted. My friend Irene and I spent our spare time in Motherwell Public Library borrowing books on Impressionism, Post Impressionism, German Expressionism. By the time we were filling in our last months at school we had flirted with Surrealism, even Dada. We thought Cubism too cold, too formal, too mathematical, altogether felt more of an emotional empathy with the line which followed Matisse out of Impressionism, rather than the one which sprang from Cézanne. But we hated the

123

mess of American Abstract Expressionism—what had Jackson Pollock been playing at? Scribbles. Dribbles. And yet to think that only a year ago we'd thought gooey pink Renoirs were the greatest thing ever painted, so who knew we might end up Pollock fans yet. Friday nights we listened to the Record Library Recording of *Under Milk Wood* with Richard Burton, we tried in vain to develop a taste for Jazz, we talked about Art School, what we'd wear, we looked at *Honey* magazines and imagined ourselves with asymmetrical haircuts and kinky boots. It was the mid sixties and things were just about to swing. Especially for us. We dreamed of beautiful bearded men who'd rescue us from the boredom and humiliation of staying in on Saturday nights. I gazed into the mirror and made self-portrait after self-portrait of myself in my version of the style of Modigliani, whom I was keen on at the time.

I dyed my hair a startling blonde with some spray on concoction that lightened as it brightened as it set, grew my fringe to nosetip level, peered through it with eyes fashionably ringed with the burnt cork effect of black eye pencil and lashbuilder mascara, asked my mother did she think I looked like Marianne Faithful at all? Irene and I took to black stockings and elastic-sided suede bootees, were engaged in a lot of tiresome arguments with the lady adviser about uniform and maintaining standards. It was grey skirts only and if that was supposed to be charcoal then it was so dark a charcoal as to be practically black. We were going downhill fast. We got into trouble for laughing while a lady from Army Recruiting was giving us a Careers Talk. We couldn't wait to leave.

It dragged itself on and on, that last year. Until finally the last day, the day I'd been longing for when I could tell all those teachers exactly what I thought of them. But of course it was easy in the relief to let half-maudlin nostalgia take over before you'd even left the place, sitting in Motherwell Town Hall at the last Prizegiving Day looking at the rows of teachers in Academic gowns and the rows of parents in flowery hats; singing 'Who would true valour see'; sniggering for the last time up the sleeves of our Banner blue-blouses at the bad grammar of the local councillor convenor. (Seventeen and snobbish, we could swallow a platitude any time and not bat an eyelid—but one thing our education had done was provide us, we thought, with a litmus for the glaringly ungrammatical, and without any sympathy for the feelings of those we regarded as less fortunate than ourselves either.)

124

So I shook hands with my teachers on the way out, thanked them even if I mumbled it and contented myself with throwing away my school tie under the cars at Motherwell Cross.

Freedom. And if I'd any complaints about the next bit, the Art School, then I'd only myself to blame. It was my own choice.

TREVOR ROYLE

The Children in the Apple Tree

At the source of the longest river
The voice of the hidden waterfall
And the children in the apple-tree
Not known, because not looked for
But heard, half-heard, in the stillness
Between two waves of the sea.

T. S. Eliot   *Little Gidding*

I knew that he was going to hit me even before the blow came. My feeble attempts to avoid the issue by argument had failed to impress him and there could be only one solution. His small muscle-packed body tensed and he hit me with a sickening punch to the head. For the first time in my young life seeing stars stopped being a comic book illusion. Another punch hit me, and another, and my attempts to stop them were like a frigate taking on a pocket battleship. I was out-gunned and out-flanked and both of us knew it.

But I had enough gumption not to cry. It was bad enough being beaten but to have cried too would have been unthinkable and in any case would only have attracted further retribution. Satisfied that the fight as any sort of competition was over my assailant lost interest and left me alone to pick myself up and to consider my crime. I was English, lah-di-dah, useless, toffee-nosed, had spoken out of turn. Even if those thoughts were not in my nine-year old head the pounding fists had certainly made the point.

Amidst my not inconsiderable pain and confusion I slowly became aware of two blue-rinsed, matinée-hatted ladies tut-tutting their disapproval of fighting in public, especially outside the Town Kirk. I looked to them for sympathy, but their frosty stare told me that I was as guilty as my attacker who was by then scuffing his way down the main street.

Two weeks later, at my first school in Scotland the lesson had been learned. An insult, real or imaginary, it didn't matter which, was thrown in my face. This time I knew what to do. A sudden fight and my taunter was so bewildered by the ferocity of my on-slaught that victory in the morning break made me a hero by four o'clock. I was one of the lads, could use my fists in a fight, could be made a member of the gang dignified by a circle of chanting boys.

Not bad for an Englishman.

You could be forgiven for thinking that that little scene had its origins in a deprived post-Industrial-Revolution urban centre. That would no doubt have been a more realistic scenario than the place where it really did happen—in St Andrews, a cold douce wee town in East Fife that would have been just like any other small Scottish town but for the dignity of its past and its university, both of which dominated the place to an exceptional degree.

St Andrews was not my home town, indeed I doubt that it ever will be. The journey from stranger to native lasts at least fifty years and unless your family is rooted in the neighbourhood, you are a newcomer. When we first went there I had spent most of my life in the Far East and my family had had little contact with post-war Britain. The world was white and those who were white were English. I am certain that I had never heard of Scotland or if I had, I probably thought of it as being a remote northern county of England. We came home (that lovely colonial euphemism for the long-lost country of one's youth) to my parent's glum separation; my father retired to his native England and my mother, brother and myself went to St Andrews where we had relatives who like us were strangers to the place. It was another world.

In the 1950s St Andrews was a very different sort of place than the busy town it is today. There was a train service but no Tay Road Bridge and the motor car had not then gained its universal ascendancy. It was a curiously remote town, not quite the same as the rest of Fife and yet firmly set on the edge of the rich farmlands of its Howe. Its history overshadowed the locality and everywhere one looked were the symbols of Scotland's past, a heritage so rich that it was easy to forget that St Andrews had languished for two centuries, a poor, church-ridden fishing town like many another East Coast neighbour.

The nineteenth century had been the town's salvation. The rise of a Scots bourgeoisie left a growing and rejuvenated medieval university and a summer holiday trade to be serviced. It was mainly a town of shopkeepers and hoteliers and remained so until it became a dormitory for the mobile professional middle classes of Dundee. There was (and is) very little poverty. Most people solidly voted Unionist and paid lip service to Scotland at countless Burns Suppers and St Andrews Nights Dinners. When I first went there, it soon became quite clear what the future would hold. The only way to get on would be to get out. 'Getting on' was the key phrase. It dominated my childhood and it was constantly dinned into me. There was a new world out there for the asking if you were prepared to work for it. I went to school (the local school, Madras College with its hungover Victorian pretensions to being a 'public' school) in the knowledge that work was all important, it being the only key to progress. Work to learn, work to understand what work means, work to know what authority is, what standards of behaviour and belief I had to respect. The primary means of learning were teaching by rote up to the age of eleven and I only have to hear the sonorous litanies of the eleven times table, a class conjugating in unison or the deliberate spelling of a-c-c-o-m-m-o-d-a-t-i-o-n to be taken back to the chalky atmosphere of a form-filled classroom. The school had been founded in 1832 by Andrew Bell, a local boy who had made good by going out to India and collecting a small fortune. Of course, he went as a chaplain and did good works but that did not seem to have deterred him from making money too. He founded the monitorial system of education whereby the pupils themselves would be responsible for disseminating instruction at elementary level and for maintaining discipline.

'Give me twelve children and in twenty-four hours I shall give you twelve teachers.'

One hundred and twenty years had done an awful lot to dilute those fine ideals and the £120,000 that had financed them, and by 1956 Madras was part of the state system of education.

The children who went to Madras in the 1950s were divided into two groups—those who would do the 'Highers' and those who would not. There was a simple dividing line—the 'qualie' (qualifying exam or 11+)—which separated innocent eleven-year-olds into As and Bs, and apart from one or two promotions and relegations along the line those were the divisions for the six years we were to spend at secondary school. If you belonged to the 'A's the road of classics and science beckoned as far as the Golden Gates of the university. It was a quiet, solid, orderly road with few

128

worries if, like myself, you kept to the middle. On the verges there were surprises, some pleasant, such as prizes, medals and a name on the dux board; others less so and primrose-covered at that.

For most of us the reward had been determined as a place at the university and preferably at the local university which occupied such a massive physical presence in the town. Even the spire of St Salvator, the university chapel, outstripped that of the Town Kirk in its praise of an all—providing and omnipresent deity. The red-gowned students, black-robed professors, examination results in the local paper and the names of departments on the doors of quiet town houses were all a constant reminder of where the brightest and best of us would eventually go to complete our educations. But the students—thae students—seemed not to work but to have fun. Charities week, the Kate Kennedy Procession, the red-gowned Sunday walk to the end of the pier were all part of an unknown and mysterious world. The students spoke with different accents too and it was only when I was older that I realised that this was because the majority were in fact English. Which was confusing for a boy who was trying to do the right and proper thing by losing his own anglicised voice. I had just to take it for granted that everyone would acquire a wondrous new accent on going to university.

The University at St Andrews has often been described as second only to Oxbridge, and sometimes less politely as a haven for those who have to put up with it as a second choice. St Andrews certainly has the appearance, but the reality is often less than kind. Anyone who has stood in the face of a North-East gale with the wind gusting down from the northern polar wastes could ever compare the town with southern England in springtime. Where there is light in the south, there is sombreness and moderation in St Andrews. An English spring is always a surprise and a revelation, it impress the northerner with its rich and sleepy beauty, but in Scotland the winter slowly gives way to a grudging summer. It is a country made for autumn. The big sky to the west over Drumcarrow Craig, a fiery pitch of red reaching up to the golden upper layers of clouds and finally giving way to the blue of night, could never belong to the south. Autumn was the season that flattered St Andrews and bathed it in a rich melancholy which suited it perfectly.

As every schoolboy amongst us knew, the first college of Scotland's oldest university was founded in 1411 as a strong beacon of learning in the north by the wealthy Bishop Wardlaw of St Andrews. It is Scotland's oldest and proudest university and yet, sadly, it has paid so little attention over the years to the land that nurtured it. St Andrews was and still is an English academic isle set in a Scottish sea. Perhaps it is too pretty a place, too reminiscent of Academe with its gracious quadrangle of St Salvator and the dainty chapel of St Leonard, too much like a collegiate university. Whatever the reason there are those who claim that it has sold its birthright too cheaply. At the time, I was innocent of such niceties and was much more concerned with the not insignificant problems of being an English boy in a predominantly Scottish school.

If the beginnings of my self-knowledge had their roots in my opening my mouth once too often then final acceptance was reached by learning a new tongue. The language surprised me. It was English undoubtedly, but of a sort, and it sounded strange and coarse to my ears. I was continually teased because I had a natural difficulty in saying 'loch' with the firm guttural sound needed to choke out the 'och'. In time this was to improve, to my own great joy but to my mother's consternation. Other words had to be learned and accepted.

'Aye' for yes, 'stanes' for stones, 'chuck' for throw, 'dyke' for wall, 'winnock' for window, 'smatter' for smash.

'Rin for it, lads he's done it noo, the great gomeril. Here comes the polis.'

Like all children we had one language for the playground and one for the classroom. Some of the farmers' sons refused to honour even that distinction and used the East Fife tongue inside and outside school, paying concessions to no one. I soon built up a set of credentials that gave me further passports and passwords. I knew how to play chickie-mellie and chappie-knockie without being caught. I could jump well at peevers (playing hoppie-restie, of course) and I came to know the intricate rules needed for playing dodge-ba' and king-ba' in a crowded playground.

By the time I got to secondary school I had learned enough to get by and to survive and, more importantly from a child's point of view, to merge into the background. I remained on the outside, keen to get on but not willing to involve myself too deeply. I could never (and this *was* a test) feel the intense dismay and dislike of the English that my friends felt. And why should I have,

130

being one myself? No matter how hard I tried, my innate (to my fellows soft) southern background betrayed me. I even felt my too obvious name to be some sort of treason and longed for the simplicity of a more usual name. I knew when it was necessary to hold my tongue and surely that is the supreme English vice?

Not that as schoolchildren there was any deep understanding of Scotland, her past, her traditions and her possibilities. North Sea Oil was still in the future and loyalties to Scotland owed more to Jimmy Shand and to the White Heather Club than to any social or political reality. That that should have been the case was partly due to the education system which was then rooted in the idea that a complete education based on the classics with a grounding in the sciences was the key that opened all doors. In their approach our teachers were more like the old village dominies who turned out lads o'pairts, pupils who had a solid factual grounding in the arts and sciences. Men like Thomas Chalmers, Duncan MacLaren or Thomas Guthrie, the great social reformers of the nineteenth century. In case any of my old teachers read this, let me say that I make this comparison not out of criticism, but out of an understanding of what they were trying to do. It was we, their pupils, who were out of sympathy and growing away too quickly from a kind of Scotland that was gradually fading into memory.

But of Scotland's real past we knew little. Culloden was the necessary and probably deserved putting down of a rebellion against authority. Gaelic was a dead language spoken by the people killed at Culloden. The Clearances were part of the world movement of peoples. Bagpipe music was the school band. The Industrial Revolution was a good thing that gave work to all those Highlanders who had gone down to Glasgow. Maclean and Maxton? Didn't they play for Third Lanark? There was no essential grounding in the political facts of Scotland's past, no intellectual debate or analysis about what had happened, why it had happened and what might be done to prevent it from happening again. We knew more about the Risorgimento than we did about the Land League resistance on Skye.

Sport gave the best clue to patriotic feelings for Scotland and provided a national focus, especially when Scotland played England at football or at rugby. Then there was an overt necessity for the men in blue not only to defeat the white-shirted hard men of England but also to thrash them, to humiliate them and to outplay

131

them with skill and arrogant superiority. The first game I ever saw at Hampden ended in a 1-1 draw (1960, the year before that terrible defeat, and disgrace for Frank Haffey), and in the dying seconds I knew what the braying crowd would choose if they were offered a second goal for Scotland or instant independence. Sure, self-government would be grand, but what could ever top the sweetness of victory over England, the Auld Enemy? It would have been Bannockburn all over again. The football writers went daft at that time of the year and sport and history mingled to make heroes of the players. Big Geordie Young, a second Bruce (Gallant Scotland defeat England's might); Billy Wright the Hammer of the Scots (Unlucky Scots fall to England's might).

Madras was a rugby-playing school albeit not a very distinguished one. The idea that football should be played as well had been discussed in the twenties but had been dismissed as a silly season aberration. Nevertheless it was the game that dominated most of our childhoods in one way or another. We supported teams which to us were only names, played twenty-a-side football on the damp corporation park on Saturday afternoons, headers against walls, kicking tennis balls along pavements and endless games of keepie-uppie and three and in. As far as I can remember there was no social differentiation about playing football or rugby and most of us played both, rugby for a school team in the morning and football for our enjoyment in the afternoon.

The greatest test though was at rugby and it came every second year at Murrayfield when Scotland played England (Wales and Ireland one year, France and England the next). Although it was expected of all of us to support Scotland with an undying devotion I cannot remember ever going to a match wholeheartedly expecting Scotland to win. Neither did many of my friends and we would sit gloomily in the train to Edinburgh forecasting yet another miserable defeat. Except against England. Then it was all bravado with myself keeping a wary silence or sporting a cocky indifference. It didn't matter who had won—on the return journey either I had to stifle my joy or I joined in the general despondency. Scotland never seemed to win in the fifties.

Looking back, I am sure that those were the heights of nationalism for me to climb and yet they were such gentle foothills that it would be wrong to give a bleak picture of a childhood spent in isolation because I had been, so to speak, born on the wrong side of the blanket. It would be convenient and perhaps half truthful to say that there was a sense of duality in my childhood. Living in Scotland, English but half Scottish and yet orphaned from the country to the south. Every year when my brother and I were dispatched to England to spend summer holidays with relatives a curious transformation took place. When we were in Scotland we were inescapably English, but in the south the mantle of the Scot was thrust upon us. Despite our surnames we were 'Scotties' or 'Jocks' and people smiled at the way we rolled our 'r's (how I tired of that sly joke). After a week or two we became more Scottish than the Scots and in the absence of critical countrymen arrogantly boasted about our adopted country's superiority. I was constantly aware that Scotland was a different place and my links with both countries only served to make the disparities more clearly and sharply defined. I grew to understand my friends' gut reactions to England and their feelings of inadequacy when they looked back at the two centuries of political partnership between the two countries. The Union of 1707 had been an awkward way of doing things and many Scots still smarted with shame at the nature of the joining together of the two very different peoples.

My English relatives certainly didn't see it in that light and it was here that the Scotch comic had made such a mark on the British imagination. Scotland for the rest of my family was a country of quaint, hairy-kneed and parsimonious old men who went about muttering into their whisky: 'It's a braw bricht moonlicht nicht the nicht, ye ken.' Such smiling small talk was calculated to bring out in me feelings of intense moral indignation which never failed to amuse my uncles and aunts. I always rose to the bait, too.

At another level, living in Scotland was socially acceptable: it was like coming up from the country or having cousins in Devon —far enough away not to be an embarrassment and yet possessed of a rural respectability. There were too the memories of a superior Scottish education, a hangover from the days of the nineteenth century when it was the Scots who helped to administrate, police and govern an English world Empire. My father's family, a respectable middle class Lancashire manufacturing family who had made their fortune in the early years of this century by the supreme Victorian virtue of industry, felt that my brother and I must be in good hands if we were at a Scottish school. If our accents had changed somewhat, well that too was no bad thing as didn't some quite acceptable people not have a slight brogue?

For the rest of my school life I merged into a reasonably happy atmosphere of contentment and well-being. In those quiet days of the fifties and early sixties there was little noticeable social unrest or urban violence, kidnappings or hijackings, inflation or bankruptcy, and yet by our own complacency we were busy sowing their seeds. Because it was such a quiet and cut-off little place St Andrews shielded most of us from the crude outside world. There were times when I sensed that something bigger and bolder was going on elsewhere and that knowledge attracted and appalled me at the same time. After my first visit alone to Europe when I was sixteen I knew that I wanted to leave that warm haven, that my young muscles needed to be flexed and tried out. I made a point of telling myself and my friends that once I left school Scotland would no longer be able to hold me.

You might ask how fifteen years later I still find myself in Scotland, married with three sons about to go the same gait as me when several disbelieving schoolfriends are scattered over the distant parts of the globe. St Andrews is after all only sixty odd miles from Edinburgh but the distance that I find myself from it now cannot be measured in man-made miles. I was grateful to the place for its security, its smallness and despite the weather its shy warmth. The education I received was sound in an old-fashioned way; it taught me little in any kind of depth but instead cluttered up my mind with obscure facts that I occasionally find useful for solving crossword puzzles. I was also taught self-confidence, and the unhappiness that I felt at the loss of my father was compensated for by the several friendships I made as a child and by my general liking for the town and the sleepy countryside that surrounded it.

But my real education began when I left St Andrews and that is what separates me from my past. I read voraciously, rediscovered Scotland, her past, and began to see through the romantic myths and legends that covered up Scotland's history and perpetuated divisions among the people. I realised that if there was to be any hope for the future the evils of the past had to be recognised and in a specifically Scottish context (to which my childhood bound me) that required an understanding of Scotland's relationship to England. This was not a neurotic concern, but I believed that it needed a better explanation than the memory of a small English boy being duffed up merely because he spoke

134

differently. Today I think I understand more about the effects of that connection—the Union of 1707, the effects of the Industrial Revolution and the continuing grip of an international capitalism, the cultural sell-out of Scottish standards. These are of course no longer directly related to the alliance but they were spawned by it. Without wanting to be pedantic, because I knew none of this at school, its revelation in maturer years was all the more telling. I am not denying that these problems are unique to Scotland but perhaps it is only in understanding one's own past first, that one becomes aware of the general human condition, or as Gramsci, the Italian Marxist, paraphrased it:

'Self-knowledge and knowledge of one's historical rights and duties do not come spontaneously, but by intelligent reflection, first by a few and then by the whole class on why certain conditions exist and how best to convert the facts of vassalage into the signals of rebellion and social reconstruction.'

My formal education taught me one set of facts and my later education taught me not only about Scotland but (in doing so) also much about contemporary politics and the ways in which politics impinge themselves upon the lives of ordinary people.

From my present vantage point, almost half-way through the hoped-for allotted span, I can see that, in a sense, you can choose your own nationality. It is not a matter of blood, despite the grim nationalism of many Scots of my generation who keep alive a selfish feeling for the country for its emotional impact alone. It is too easy to summon up the half-true, half-phoney romantic spirit of long lost battles, or football matches, the two blending together so easily, against the Auld Enemy. By learning about the real past and the political conditions of their own country it may be that Scots at school today will have a greater compassion for the dispossessions and political imbalances in other further flung parts of the world. Scotland can become another country and, like the past, a different one from the place I knew as a child. There are other reasons too why I decided to stay in Scotland. I like it here, so does my family. Scotland is a country I grew to love as a child, and we feel at home in the north—it is as simple and domestic as that.

And yet underlying that complacency is the terrible sense of paradox in Scotland. On the one hand I can feel a strong empathy with a small country with its own indigenous culture being threat-

135

ened by the processes of international big business. On a rational and political level that is comprehensible. On the other I have experienced a people torn by several emotions unable to express itself formally and yet in frightening detail able to display the whole gamut of passionate experience from extremes of anguished love to extremes of bitter violence. There were times when I felt that my forebears must have landed with St Regulus to plant the bones of the crucified saint and so give the town its name, such was my joy of St Andrews and my sense of acceptance by it. There were also those infrequent times, dark to the memory, when I bitterly resented the shame of being on the outside and cursed the Scots bigotry towards the English and all that they stood for. In Scotland there can be no middle way.

On the evening before I left St Andrews to go to another university in another part of the country I had gone drinking with a few friends to celebrate the parting of the ways. Walking back home after closing time we passed a group of Freshers who were waiting to go up to St Andrews University. Like us they were flushed with drink and new-found freedom. We heard them coming before they staggered into sight—loud braying English voices magnified by too many pints of beer. As they passed a group of local hoods standing outside the one café that kept late hours, to our horror, a scuffle broke out. One of the students fell with a well-aimed butt to the head and as he went down the boot went in.

As a piece of violence it was hardly remarkable and it was over in seconds. The lads sauntered off with scarcely a glance in our direction and the hapless Englishman was left to pick himself up and to consider his crime. As his assailant passed us he spat into the gutter and sneered: 'English student shite.'

The following day I went down to the station and left behind me the town that I had known for so long. There was to be no return.

GILES GORDON

The Thrie Estaitis: Scotch, Scots, Scottish

I was educated at the Edinburgh Academy. So was my father. So
was his father. Maybe *his* father was too. My sons are unlikely to
be educated there, if only because we live in London, not the least
of the reasons for that being that it wouldn't be possible for me
to earn anything approaching what I do—as a writer and literary
agent—in any other city in the British Isles, and that includes the
capital of Scotland.

During the fifties, when I was at the Academy as a day boy,
about 200 pupils out of just under 1,000 were boarders. If my
wife and I were planning to send our sons to boarding school,
which we're not, my old school would hardly be top of the list:
it's not a proper boarding school. (Also, I think that if, as a
grown-up person, you inflict your progeny on the world or the
world on your progeny it is less than playing the game in their
formative years to farm your children out to others, night and
weekends as well as during the day.) We day boys—the school
was no more co-educational then than presumably it is now—regarded the boarders as a race apart, mostly English or their parents
beyond the Forth, shoring up the remnants of Empire. It wasn't
quite proper not to be brought up in the bosom of the Presbyterian
family; the housemasters, their wives and charges hardly classified
as extended families. I remember the boarders possessing, like
Cassius, a lean and hungry look. They *were* skinnier than we day
boys, better than we were at those traditional Scottish games,
rugby and cricket, more likely than the rest of us to become n.c.o.'s
in the Combined Cadet Force. They tended to dress scruffily except
on Mondays when, inexplicably, they would be the best turned
out cadets on parade with the highest shine on their brasses, the
most glistening toe-caps, and the least blanco where blanco
shouldn't have been. It was obligatory to take part in the cadet
force then. Battledress trousers were worn in the winter, kilts in

137

the summer and at the week's annual camp. Being born in May 1940 I was among the first lot to miss compulsory national service. Still, Lieutenant Booth, the biology master, taught me how to dismantle a bren gun although I always had one bit left over after I'd put it together again.

Our children go to schools where they aren't obliged to wear uniform—couldn't, if they wished to do so. They look like themselves. Their clothes reflect their characters, and that of their parents. It has always seemed to me one of the ironies and paradoxes of the Academy that though it and other public schools, major and minor, in Edinburgh and elsewhere (yes, including England), seek to turn out potential leaders of their fellow men and women those leaders manqué are obliged to dress identically in cap, blazer, tie, trousers (what, no kilt?), socks, shoes. The letters EA were embroidered on the blazer pocket within a silver laurel wreath—perhaps the one the mighty Julius just failed to accept from Antony? The school motto was in Latin, Homer's head the crest and Greek regularly on the agenda; the school's neoclassical aspirations were not in doubt. I still experience a frisson of alarm and Scottish guilt when I pass a well-groomed man walking along Piccadilly sporting the old school tie. Alarm, because it's depressing to contemplate that any adult has had such little satisfaction in life subsequent to his school days that he chooses to display such an emblem of adolescence and conformity. Guilt, that I'm not playing the game and wearing a similar tie, which I'd be entitled to do if I paid the Academical Club annual subscription. A few years ago one man in a hundred in London appeared to be an Edinburgh Academical. Woolworths, I think it was, were selling a near identical tie.

It could be argued, frequently is, that public schools in Scotland —by which of course are meant private schools where money is supposed to be able to buy you a superior education, or at least teach you to how to behave as a gentleman—have more to do with that part of Britain below the belt of the Tweed and the British imperialist ethos than they do with Scotland, and that is not a point I'd want to dispute. What I would assert is that each year tens of thousands of young men and women are educated in such establishments north as well as south of the Border, and that their later attitude towards their native land is substantially derived from their experience at these schools, and what they are taught and not taught there.

138

Lord Cockburn was one of those responsible for the foundation of the neo-classical Edinburgh Academy, and so was Sir Walter Scott. Robert Louis Stevenson, described in a recent biography as an 'indifferent schoolboy', was a pupil. You can't, presumably, get much more Scottish than those three.

And yet, and yet . . . The only time throughout all my years at the Academy I encountered the name of Robert Burns was when Lord Cameron, the then chairman of the governors, presented me at the annual prize-giving in 1955 with a cheap edition—published by Collins of Glasgow—of the poems and songs as a music prize. (Which is another story, as to this day I cannot read a note of music. The principals in the bi-annual Gilbert and Sullivan production—the alternate years being taken up with a Shakespeare play—were invariably awarded Ernest R. Balfour music prizes. My boyish voice—of which the *Edinburgh Academy Chronicle* reported: 'It was indeed a rare piece of good fortune to have available so true and accomplished an alto, and Gordon certainly rose to the occasion'—was in the process of breaking the very week I sang the Queen of the Fairies in *Iolanthe* opposite Gordon Honeycombe's Private Willis. Years later we found ourselves as authors on the same publisher's list, Hutchinson, the managing director of which, Charles Clark, had been head ephor (that is, being translated from the Greek, prefect of the Academy during my first year in the upper school. Either he or Honeycombe, and it's curious I can't recall which as they looked as little alike then as they do now, had in the early fifties presented me with a judicial beating on the shiny seat of my shorts. They were both school ephors, and entitled to wallop other boys for trivial misdemeanours. I had been seen by someone presumably in authority in the streets of Edinburgh eating a lollipop whilst wearing school uniform. The instrument of punishment was a clacken, a wooden bat resembling a large, flat spoon which was otherwise used for playing the ridiculous school game, hailes, the object of which was to strike a small ball with a clacken into the opposing team's goal.)

But to revert to Burns. Having shaken Lord Cameron's hand and the applause having died down, I opened the book not at the time wondering what Rabbie would have felt about having Homer's head in profile and in gold stamped on the cover of his work. I read the introduction and with some embarrassment learned that Burns had fifteen children, nine being born in 'lawful wedlock'. Before I had time to wonder where that left the other six it was reassuring to read in the next sentence that 'in no sense was Burns a libertine'. Undoubtedly a Scot of whom his fellows could be proud. I looked at the photographs of The Burns Country which followed the introduction. They were of such places as Alloway, Ayr, Dumfries and Kilmarnock, names I had seen on maps of Scotland and two of which I identified as football teams: not places that had anything to do with my life. I then came to the poems and songs. I found, with some puzzlement, that I couldn't with ease or pleasure—in fact only with difficulty and constant recourse to the glossary—read them. Burns was Scottish, I was Scottish, yet he didn't write in the language I'd been brought up, at home and at school, to speak and read. If he meant 'such' why did he write 'sic'; why 'streekit' for 'stretched'; why 'gae' for 'go'; 'leddy' for 'lady'; 'tocher' for 'dowry'? Then I wondered why I should try, why I should make the effort. After all, I could read Shakespeare, and Scott (except some of the dialogue) and RLS, even Chaucer, and they—the Scots as well as the English—wrote in English and English was the language of English literature, wasn't it? And English literature included Scottish literature, didn't it?

I hope my present reader will not write off the above paragraphs as simple snobbery or elitism. On the contrary, I mean to suggest—quite humbly—that not being able to read Burns with a sense of fulfilment at the age of fifteen was a singular deprivation, and one from which I haven't fully recovered. I do not know if the Edinburgh Academy and similar institutions yet teach Scottish literature, but if they don't it's a shaming indictment of the system and of the country. Not the least of the problems twenty years or longer ago was that few of the staff were Scottish, and I can't recall one such who taught English. Why should—how could—an English English master teach Scottish literature? I remember the hilarity in class once when an English English master who also taught history (and opened the batting more than once for the Scottish national cricket team) tried to explain that the Battle of Pinkie could best be remembered by thinking of a pink eye. He'd never heard of a pinkie. The masters who had been born Scottish were, by education, brain-washing and ultimately inclination, as English as the English. The rector, Scots by birth, taught us *Kidnapped*, chapter by chapter, week by week, for two years (not terms) in succession. The second year we went back to chapter one although by the end of the previous year we hadn't reached the last chapter of the short novel. It was symbolic of the attitude of Scottish public schools that the ultimate academic goal for pupils was not the Scottish Higher Leaving Certificate but the Oxford and Cambridge 'A' Level Examinations. At the Academy, it was the less bright boys who sat the Highers.

*

As a child, one is conditioned as much by one's home life as by one's school, or more so. My father was, and is, an architect of some reputation and honour, with an office in Heriot Row in the New Town. My brother (four years younger than me), my sister (four years younger than him) and I were brought up in what in the forties and fifties was, with a certain precision, thought of as a middle class household. Not everyone then was middle class as they are now, with the exception of the odd peer of the realm. We lived first at Churchill, then at Bruntsfield, and regarded Morningside as terribly refined and genteel. My mother, who was brought up in Northern Ireland, was a professional pianist before marriage, and it was hoped that we children would be musical. My brother and sister were—two instruments apiece but taught privately, not at school—I wasn't. I used to dread the annual concert given by the Waddell Junior Orchestra at the Assembly Rooms in George Street, with my brother or sister usually playing a solo.

As children we weren't encouraged to play much with other children. On the other hand we weren't discouraged. The geographical circumstances of a middle class childhood—detached or semi-detached houses with gardens and hedges or stone walls and almost definitely few other children in the street—tend to force the child, when not at school, on to his own resources. We had few friends, and perhaps friendship even today means less to me than it should. I turned to the printed word, ate paper and drank ink voraciously. There were hundreds of books in the house, and at an early age I became a Saturday morning habitué of the Morningside Public Library. I wonder if there are still as many books there as there were then by my favourites, Conan Doyle and Baroness Orczy? I rarely if ever read 'Scottish' books, though my father had Scottish history on his shelves and books about Scottish architecture.

Summer holidays were usually spent either in England, as often studying cathedrals and historic towns as lying on a beach, or abroad: the (then) continent of Europe. My father was architect to the High Kirk of St Giles as well as being a Church of Scotland elder there. He would don his striped trousers and head waiter's coat each Sunday morning, and we would spend an hour and a half beneath the tattered flags of the so-called Cathedral singing hymns and psalms and prose psalms and paraphrases (there never seemed a logical difference between them) and closing our eyes whilst interminable prayers were spoken or read, and listening to the exquisite mandarin English of the Dean of the Thistle, Dr Warr, a man of stature who, unlike his successor as minister, was prepared to play the Church of Scotland game by the rules. Once upon a time there was a man called John Knox. Once upon a time there was a woman called Mary Stewart or Stuart. Her entry in *The Concise Dictionary of National Biography* is substantially larger than his but there's no doubt that the divine had and continues to have greater influence on his fellow countrymen and women than the queen ever did.

The heart of the matter is now reached; and will not go away. This is where the individual Scottish upbringing and education merges with that of the education and upbringing of every Scot, where—even—Edinburgh becomes Glasgow, the Lowlands the Highlands, the three estaits one, Protestant Roman Catholic. I was taught Scottish history for two or three years at school, the lessons now in my mind being accompanied as they were then in the text books by William Hole's graphic representations of the big set-pieces of Scottish history, featuring kings in triumph, people in adversity. Holy writ was Hume Brown's witless and inelegant prose; but the facts were there, they certainly were. The print in school histories of Scotland seemed to be smaller than the print in other history books: was this because the subject was important, therefore no palliative for the reader was appropriate, or because there was so much essential history to be got through that the only way to cope between the covers of one book was to keep the size of the type right down? Either way. I've been suspicious since of books set in tiny type, not to mention the damage they do to the eyes.

The Edinburgh Academy ceased to teach Scottish history once the Upper School was reached, at the age of thirteen or thereabouts. At the time, it seemed to me that the point about Scottish history—and not just at the *1314 and All That* level—was that everyone came to a sticky end, that for the Scot everything went wrong sooner rather than later. Even Wallace and Bruce, folk heroes par excellence, proved all too mortal, not to mention both young and old pretenders. The history as well as the Lowlands weather seemed relentlessly grey, the only other relevant colour being gore. From Mons Graupius onwards, culminating in the Act of Union and certainly taking in such empirical episodes as the Darien Scheme and the South Sea Bubble, it was closer to farce than tragedy. The Scot lacks a sense of humour to the extent he does and as the word is generally understood because he cannot afford to possess one. Faced with John Knox and Mary Queen of Scots in your history the only appropriate response, if you're to remain sane, is either to hoot with laughter or to weep. Instead, the Scot twitches and shuffles, the divided self triumphs, moral ambiguity rules, Hogg's Justified Sinner, Deacon Brodie, Jekyll and Hyde, and R. D. Laing are the touchstones.

I'm still far from certain whether John Knox and Mary are more appropriately regarded as the Adam and Eve of Scotland, the couple responsible for our subsequent woes, the national neuroses and masochism, or as the Punch and Judy, a knockabout turn kept in the repertoire for the edification of visitors, the sugar on the shortbread, the salt in the porridge, the drone in the bagpipes. Are they, is their inheritance, the real Scotland—or an escape from facing up to it and its attendant problems? The Scot prides himself in being a realist but, in spite of Kirk-o'-Field, there has been a slow fuse burning for more than 400 years from the gunpowder keg that is Mary and Knox. It must be blown up, mourned and forgotten before the country can in the last quarter of the twentieth century regain its pride within Britain, within Europe.

At school, everyone seemed to assume that Knox was the baddie, Mary the goodie—in spite of their respective personalities, politics, religion, stance; and yet Knox was and remains the country's household god. I remember the feeling of guilt enshrined in my body, nagging at mind and conscience, when, in my early teens, I queued outside the Assembly Hall at the top of the Mound one Festival to see *The Thrie Estaitis*: the finger-pointing graven image of John Knox high on his pedestal in the courtyard was watching me, and—oh, brother!—did he disapprove of my going to the theatre, and in a building that was historically the home of the Church of Scotland General Assembly!

Whether I genuinely felt this at the time, which I believe I did, or whether I was the victim of the Edinburgh mass media, of prejudice and disapproval expressed from pulpit and letters to the editor, is not the point. The fundamental question is: *why* does the fact of being a Scot fill us (you, me) with such a sense of guilt? And what is this guilt, imbibed with our mother's milk and to which we're addicts years before the first drop of whisky, the other communion wine, passes our lips?

*

For more than fifteen years I've lived away from Scotland, visiting Edinburgh at most once a year. The night before I left the capital in the early sixties to seek my fortune in London, Sydney Goodsir Smith in the Abbotsford in Rose Street thrust his monocle into an eye and said, 'You won't come back; they never do,' and poured a half pint of heavy over my head. At the time I was quite certain that I would return to live in Edinburgh after a few years.

I feel no more English now than I did when I lived and was educated and worked in Edinburgh for four years. Indeed, I take pride in my nationality now, am aware of it. In Edinburgh I took it for granted. As a family, my parents, my brother and sister and I, were—I realise in retrospect, and in comparison with families of a roughly similar kind and background—extremely close. I took my Scottishness for granted to the extent that I did not least because my father was and remains quietly but hugely proud of being Scots, of his and the family's heritage, of the country's achievement and achievements down the centuries. He glories in his nationality, in a very positive sense; in living and working in Edinburgh, in the history and architecture and fine arts and culture of the country. He inspired within his children a sense of Scotland, of Scottishness, of the Scottish tradition, its attend-ant morality and ambiguities, of what—simply—it means in the best and most positive sense to be a Scot. He—in his modest, dignified and informed way—could be nothing but Scots. That, I believe, is the basis of his life. He feels Scots, therefore he is; or, if it be preferred, he is Scots, therefore he feels so. All this I only learned to acknowledge and respect from London, and there too I realised that there was no escape from the fact that I was as Scottish as my father.

And yet, considered in another way, I regard myself as being

144

the nationality my passport has always proclaimed me to be: British. I'd surmise that relatively few people—tens of thousands rather than millions—think of themselves as indigenously British. Certainly most of the English don't: they know they are English; the Welsh are Welsh and the Scots are Scots. Which leaves a slender majority of the Northern Irish as British.

I do not feel British because I live in London. I feel British because my Scottish education, my education in Scotland wittingly or unwittingly inculcated upon me the assets of being British. I believe fundamentally that it's a privilege to be British today (rather than, say, at the turn of the century) and certainly my bones and flesh and spirit are Scottish-British; and I repudiate any suggestion of being English-British. Admittedly my children have a more varied strain within them as my wife is that rarity, a born and bred Londoner.

As I've already said, the Scot prides himself in being a realist. This has always seemed to be the opposite of the truth. They who proclaim themselves realists rarely are. Why, oh why does the Scot (of course I include myself) have such an inferiority complex *about being Scottish?* What could be more indicative of this neurotic condition than the wearing of that bourgeois, genteel and latter-day garment, the kilt? It is a fact that Scotland receives a higher subsidy per head of population from central government in London than does any other part of the United Kingdom. Scots may resent this but why do they so regularly deny it? It must be a fact that the country would be in a worse state even than it is—economically, politically, culturally—without this subsidy. That the words and warnings of Tam Dalyell, a wise and humane human being with more understanding of what is valuable in Scotland than such mediocre minds as those of the more bigoted Scottish Nationalists, are at this time scorned and disregarded to the extent they are says little for the individual Scot's reading of his history. Very likely a greater measure of independence for 'North Britain' will be achieved, and the country be seen to govern itself from the Royal High School, and Scotland's collective ego such that when the place is as pathetic and enfeebled as is the Republic of Ireland its denizens will proclaim, without caring whether it be true or not, that they're better off than they were under the English yoke. By the time this condition is reached it will not be possible for them to say anything other.

145

It seems to me that the Scot can only function as a Scot, in the grown-up sense implied, when he leaves the country, when he forgets that John Knox and Mary Stewart or Stuart and all the other egomaniacs ever existed rather than think continually that he's cast them aside, disciplined them: 'Down, Satan, down'; when his education, his professional or other skills, his soul, his conscience his keen sense of morality, this steadfastness and integrity may be utilised elsewhere. Down the centuries many if not most of the greatest Scots have achieved fulfilment only when they've left the country. To take one contemporary example: Muriel Spark seems to me unarguably the finest living Scottish novelist. Her novels are as brilliant as they are, as complex and truthful in the way that they are, to a considerable degree *because* she was brought up and educated in Edinburgh. Is it because she's exiled in Rome that she's rarely referred to by Scottish critics as a Scottish writer? The *Observer* wrote recently of her: 'By her own account, Muriel Spark has become "more historically-minded", more interested in roots, though not in any sentimental way. She views Scottish Nationalism as sinister "folklorism": 'I'm against any nationalist movement, they're fascist ultimately —out with the English, out with the Jews." ' She, convert to Roman Catholicism, is half-Jewish.

The Scot by temperament is reductionist, the opposite of expansionist. Small may or may not be beautiful, it's certainly easier to grasp and comprehend than big. The Scot—and this his education has taught him—needs to have a ballast of facts upon which to construct his precarious identity as a Scot. He lacks not merely a fundamental and necessary self-confidence and self-respect but an understanding that he must be himself first, Scot second. The reasons for this insecurity when confronted by something which he doesn't fully comprehend are still not properly understood, and I'm not talking about humility. It's the triviality that's so mind-boggling. Why, for instance, should intelligent people expend time, energy, column metres in books and the press arguing whether Scotch, Scots or Scottish is the most correct usage? Such a discussion at this time in history has little to do with precision of thought, accuracy of expression. Why should the Scots ego be so vulnerable that whenever some British (sorry, English) journalist writes 'English' when he means 'British' we all know that a subsequent issue of the paper will contain a snide, facetious little letter pointing out that the problem with England is that it thinks Scotland a part of it? In Edinburgh a month ago a garage attendant gave my wife a Scottish pound note in change. She asked if he could possibly give her an English pound note as our next stop was south of the Border. He explained, with a minimum of humour and courtesy, that the Scots pound was legal tender in England, and if anyone refused to accept it she should summon a policeman. It's surely not merely a feeble acceptance of the status quo to wonder who in such a situation wants to summon a policeman, assuming one can be found? Admittedly the country's writers have rarely been over-endowed with a sense of humour but it's depressing (because it's symptomatic of the national malaise) to find that two middle-aged poets each with the same surname are still abusing each other as they were over a decade ago in any periodical that will publish their petty and ultimately meaningless spleen.

Must the Scot's battles of yesteryear, whether lost or won, be fought for ever? It may be objected to that these pages have little to do with my education in Edinburgh. I would disagree. They are as a result of that education, and to the majority the process of education is not primarily an end in itself. Perhaps we harbour the inferiority complex we do because, *together with* the Welsh and the people of Ulster, we equal only one fifth of the English. And yet the contribution that individual Scots have made to these islands, to the late British Empire, to the American navy and the planet Earth is incalculable. But, I passionately submit, it is those Scots who have been able to get over their superficial allegiance to the idea of their country, the high-brow haggis bashing, who have attained—most usually without being aware of the fact—a real Scottishness.

Hugh MacDiarmid wrote an essay about David Hume entitled 'The Man of (almost) Independent Mind'. How depressing that our most influential living poet should deem it appropriate to qualify his designation of our greatest philosopher by such an adverb, as if Hume were the only Scot to have possessed—possibly—a mind of his own.

Biographical Details

ALAN BOLD was born in Edinburgh in 1943 and was educated at Edinburgh University. He worked as a journalist with *The Times Educational Supplement* in Scotland before becoming a fulltime writer and painter. He has published many collections of poetry and has edited several anthologies including *The Penguin Book of Socialist Verse* and the *Cambridge Book of English Verse 1939-75*. He now lives in Markinch, Fife, with his wife Alice and daughter Valentina.

BILL BRYDEN is Associate Director of the National Theatre. He has previously worked at the Royal Court and the Royal Lyceum, Edinburgh where two of his own plays *Willie Rough* and *Benny Lynch* were produced. He has also directed plays for the Edinburgh Festival and wrote the libretto for Scottish Opera's production *Hermiston* by Robin Orr in 1976.

DONALD CAMPBELL began his writing career in the late sixties, when his first poems were published. Since then, he has worked as a poet, playwright, critic and radio script-writer. Appointed Writer-in-Residence to Edinburgh Schools in 1974, he devotes much of his time to encouraging young people to take an interest in literature. Currently, his main concern is with his plays, of which the best-known is *The Jesuit* (1976). His other books include *Poems* (1971), *Rhymes 'n Reasons* (1972) and *Murals* (1975).

CATHERINE CZERKAWSKA was born of mixed Polish, English and Irish parentage in 1951. After graduating in Medieval Studies and Folklore at the universities of Edinburgh and Leeds she is now teaching in Finland. Her collection of poems *A Book of Men* won a Scottish Arts Council Award in 1976.

GILES GORDON was indoctrinated into publishing at Oliver & Boyd, when it was still an indigenous Scottish imprint. Since then he has worked in London, his last publishing job being editorial director at Gollancz. For the last four years he has divided his time between being a literary agent and novelist, short story writer, poet and radio playwright. Married, three children.

JOHN HERDMAN was born in Edinburgh in 1941 and graduated in English at Cambridge in 1963. His published books are *Descent* (1968), *A Truth Lover* (1973), and *Memoirs of my Aunt Minnie/ Clapperton* (1974), and he has contributed to others including *Whither Scotland?* (ed. Duncan Glen, 1971). He also contributes literary criticism regularly to Scottish periodicals. He was awarded a Scottish Arts Council Bursary in 1976.

LIZ LOCHHEAD was born on Boxing Day, 1947 in Motherwell, Lanarkshire's largest steel town. After school, went to Glasgow School of Art, while contrarily becoming more and more obsessed with writing poetry. First collection, *Memo for Spring*, was published in 1972. Currently teaches in a large Glasgow comprehensive school.

MARTIN MACDONALD lives in Inverness where he is a freelance journalist and broadcaster, contributing frequently to the BBC, Grampian TV and Norwegian television. He became a journalist after graduating from Edinburgh University and later worked for the BBC as a producer in their Gaelic Department and as an editor in Aberdeen. Contributes a weekly Gaelic column to the Skye-based *West Highland Free Press*.

ALLAN MASSIE was born in Singapore in 1938. He was educated at Glenalmond and Trinity College, Cambridge. He has taught in Scotland and Italy. He writes short stories and has contributed reviews and other articles to *The Scotsman, The London Magazine, The Times Literary Supplement* and the BBC. He is at present finishing a novel and working on a study of Muriel Spark.

TREVOR ROYLE was born in India and spent his early years in the Far East. He was educated in Scotland and is presently Literature Director of the Scottish Arts Council. He has published essays and reviews in several literary magazines and in 1976 he co-edited a book about Scottish football. Married with three sons, and although born an Englishman, looks on Scotland as his home.

ALAN SPENCE is aged twenty-nine and was born and raised in Glasgow. He attended Glasgow University 1966-69 and 1973-74; in between worked at various jobs, spent time in Europe and USA, and became a disciple of Indian spiritual master Sri Chinmoy. He is married and is presently Fellow in Creative Writing at Glasgow University.

BOB TAIT, born Kilmarnock, 1943. Currently lecturer in educational studies, Aberdeen College of Education. Previously editor of *Scottish International Review*, 1967-73, and continues that side of his interests by way of current affairs broadcasts for Radio Aberdeen. National Executive member of the break-away Scottish Labour Party.